The Research Report Series of the Institute for Social Research is composed of significant reports published at the completion of a research project. These reports are generally prepared by the principal research investigators and are directed to selected users of this information. Research Reports are intended as technical documents which provide rapid dissemination of new knowledge resulting from ISR research.

RESEARCH REPORT SERIES, INSTITUTE FOR SOCIAL RESEARCH

Subjective Well-Being among Different Age Groups

A. Regula Herzog
Willard L. Rodgers
Joseph Woodworth

Survey Research Center
Institute for Social Research
The University of Michigan

1982

Final Report on Grant No. MH29747, National Institute of Mental Health

Library of Congress Cataloging in Publication Data:

Herzog, A. Regula (Anna Regula), 1941–
    Subjective well– being among different age groups.

    (Research report series / Institute for Social Research)

        Bibliography: p.
        1. Age groups. 2. Happiness. 3. Mental Health.
I. Rodgers, Willard L. II. Woodworth, Joseph, 1950–
III. Title. IV. Series: Research report series (University
of Michigan. Institute for Social Research)
HM131.H398 1982   305.2   82-12094
ISBN 0-87944-283-2 (pbk.)

ISR Code No. 9017

Published in 1982 by:
Institute for Social Research,
The University of Michigan, Ann Arbor, Michigan

6 5 4 3 2 1

Manufactured in the United States of America

Acknowledgements

This is the final report of a project sponsored by the National Institute of Mental Health on subjective well-being in older age. The project was based on data from a number of surveys most of which were originally conducted by the Survey Research Center at The University of Michigan. The grant from the National Institute of Mental Health provided funding for conducting the data analyses and for writing this report as well as two journal articles. We are greatly indebted to our staff, including Lynn Dielman and Philip Pappalardo for data management and data analysis, and Marge Dalian for secretarial assistance. We are also grateful to the principal investigators of the studies that we used for so gracefully making their data available. Among them are Frank Andrews, the late Angus Campbell, Richard Curtin, Philip Converse, Elizabeth Douvan, Robert Groves, Thomas Juster, Richard Kulka, Joseph Veroff, and Stephen Withey. These and many others of our colleagues-- among them Duane Alwin, Toni Antonucci, Graham Kalton, Melvin Manis, Sandra Newman, and Michael Sivak--gave freely of their time and expertise. Finally, this project would not have been possible without all the respondents who participated in the various surveys. We extend our thanks to all of them.

TABLE OF CONTENTS

LIST OF TABLES

ix

CHAPTER 1

INTRODUCTION

Does happiness and life satisfaction increase or decrease with age and why? When older people say that they are happy or satisfied with life, do they mean the same thing as younger or middle aged people who say that they are happy or satisfied with life? And if they are not talking about the same thing, what does this imply for efforts to answer questions about the relationship between age and happiness/life satisfaction?

Efforts to develop social indicators have stimulated interest in the issue of subjective well-being (Bradburn, 1969; Campbell et al., 1976; Andrews and Withey, 1976). However, much of this research concentrates on the population as a whole rather than on comparison of specific age groups. On the other hand, while dealing with the issue of age, the gerontological literature tends to study samples of older people with little attention paid to whether their findings represent characteristics and processes unique to older people. Thus, not enough effort has been put into systematically examining the change and development of subjective well-being across the life span.

In this collection of papers we hope to help fill in this gap by focusing attention on the age differences in subjective well-being, its structure and its predictor patterns. Although we are aware that age differences in cross-sectional data are not synonymous with the process of aging, cross-sectional data can provide a useful beginning to such investigations. Furthermore, there are currently available several sets of relevant cross-sectional data from several large representative nationwide samples, which can be usefully applied to such investigations.

We will examine the following questions: Do various age groups share a common definition of subjective well-being? Does a similar structure of dimensions of subjective well-being tend to emerge across all age groups? How is age related to subjective well-being and how might we explain this relationship? Is satisfaction with various aspects of life related similarly to global subjective well-being in all age groups? Do demographic factors likely to affect subjective well-being have similar effects across age groups? What role do activity pursuits play in enabling older people to successfully adjust to retirement?

However, before proceeding with the presentation of our analysis, we briefly review some of the previous theoretical and empirical work that provides some of the context for our interest in these questions.

Significance of subjective well-being for the understanding of human behavior

The nature of happiness lies at the heart of human existence and as such has occupied philosophers for centuries. Plato's Symposium comes readily to mind; and in the fifth century Augustine referred to some 300 philosophical definitions of happiness that existed at his time, a number which could probably easily be multiplied if more recent thinkers were to be included. At the same time, the philosophical analysis of happiness has defied easy answers because of the eminently subjective nature of that concept.

The continuous preoccupation with the concept of happiness is undoubtedly related to its significance for the understanding of human nature. From a psychological perspective, Freud and his colleagues assigned a central role to happiness in proposing that the will for pleasure is a major motivational force behind all human endeavors. Although the basic form of pleasure was cast very much in sensual terms, Freud also believed that all attempts at attaining such pleasure were basically doomed by moral restrictions of this society and had instead to be attained in transformed form through such things as pleasure from artistic experience.

A sense of well-being has of course a focal meaning in the psychiatric definition of depression, which centers on the almost total absence of any feelings of happiness or satisfactions with life and with self. While the diagnosis of depression is only applied to people of pathologically low well-being and therefore refers to an extreme group, well-being defined in this form has been shown to have wide-spread behavioral effects. For example, persons afflicted with depressed moods tend to show a general slowing of reactions, and lessened effectiveness in providing for themselves or their families. Moreover, many depressed persons will have to be protected from harming themselves by institutionalization. In brief, an extremely low level of subjective well-being has a pervasive effect on the afflicted person's day-to-day functioning.

While psychiatric and psychoanalytical theories attribute much importance to the individual's sense of well-being, they were developed on the basis of data from persons who experience problems severe enough to require professional help. In 1957 a major study on subjective well-being among the general American population was conducted by Gurin, Veroff, and Feld (1960). As an attempt to study mental health from a positive perspective, this study showed quite clearly that even among the general population, who never showed up in a doctor's or psychiatrist's office, subjective well-being varied considerably. In other words, people seemed to differ in how good they felt about their life, and these feelings were to some degree affected by their social standing. For example, women expressed less subjective well-being than men.

More recently, a series of large-scale surveys have been conducted that focus on issues of subjective well-being and positive mental health as an outgrowth of developments in social indicators research. While early attempts to monitor the status of the nation have focused on objective indicators--such as economic or health characteristics of the population--the recognition has been growing rapidly that monitoring the population's feelings about their lives and various aspects of it is equally critical. Within this general framework, Bradburn and Caplovitz (1965) have conducted pilot studies focusing on positive mental health. Since then, Bradburn (1969) has reported on a large follow-up study to his pilot studies. The series of General Social Surveys conducted by the National Opinion Research Center since 1972 have included questions on satisfactions with various domains of life. Campbell and his colleagues (1976) have designed a set of questions probing satisfaction and implemented them in two national surveys in 1971 and 1978. And finally, Andrews and Withey (1976) have developed an extremely comprehensive set of questions on satisfactions and carefully analyzed their properties. These studies have demonstrated that subjective well-being tends to be related to many core psychological and behavioral factors, such as feelings of personal competence, contact with friends, or participation in clubs and other groups. Although the direction of causation could not be identified in cross-sectional designs like these, the studies nevertheless document the central role that subjective well-being assumes within a person's life.

Life span patterns of subjective well-being

With regard to life span patterns, happiness has always been considered a part of youth, while the shrinking perspective associated with growing older is assumed to lead to unhappiness, if not despair. On the basis of such life span assumptions, in addition to the notion that environments created by urban industrial societies are particularly hostile to older people (cf. Maddox, 1970), research on subjective well-being has assumed a predominant place in social-gerontological research. Although this research focuses largely on the aged, two types of hypotheses are usually implied: (a) subjective well-being declines with increasing age; and (b) subjective well-being in older age groups is differently affected by situational factors such as poverty, ill health, and the like because the aged are more vulnerable to such factors. However, relatively little information is available on life span patterns, and what evidence is available suggests that the two hypotheses are not true in this general a form. Regarding the first issue, happiness indeed shows a tendency to decline with age and the incidence of diagnosed depression increases, but at the same time reports of worrying decline and reported satisfactions increase (Campbell et al., 1976; Gurin et al., 1960). Apparently, different indicators do not tell the same story. Perhaps superficial adaptation improves, while deep-seated despair grows. Or, perhaps all the depressed older people refuse to respond to a survey, leaving the well-adjusted older people as the only older people willing to be interviewed. Whatever the correct explanation for the first contention may be, there is no more consistent support for the second one. Health status has a stronger impact on subjective well-being among the aged than among younger age groups according to one study (Spreitzer and Snyder, 1974), but not according to another (Palmore and Luikart, 1972); and economic situation does affect different age groups in much the same ways in one study (Spreitzer and Snyder, 1974) or the young and middle-aged even more than the old according to another study (Palmore and Luikart, 1972).

An even more preliminary issue needs to be raised in this context. Comparing various age levels assumes that the nature of the measure remains the same for different age groups. Little work is currently available to document that assumption; and the work that is available is not entirely supportive of the assumption (Andrews and Withey, 1976; Campbell et al., 1976; Cutler, 1979).

The concept of subjective well-being and its measurement

As noted above, subjective well-being--described by a multitude of definitions referring to life satisfaction, happiness, adjustment, mastery, or mental health, and measured by a plethora of devices--has remained for decades at the center of attempts to explain successful aging in social-gerontological research. In the course of this research considerable attention has been devoted to the form of appropriate measurement devices of subjective well-being for older people and thereby--implicitly more than explicitly--to the definition, meaning, and structure of the concept amongst older people, (For a recent summary and critique of these efforts see Nydegger, 1977.)

One of the most widely used scales for measuring subjective well-being is the Life Satisfaction Index A developed by Neugarten, Havighurst and Tobin (1961) for use in the Kansas City Study. The scale consists of a set of items designed to tap a number of components thought to be part of a general life satisfaction or morale concept--Zest for Life; Resolution and Fortitude; Congruence between Desired and Achieved Goals; Positive Self-concept; and Mood Tone. Investigations of the measurement qualities of the scale (Adams, 1969; Neugarten et al., 1961) have suggested satisfactory reliability and validity. Adams' (1969) work further confirmed that one major factor accounted for most of the variance thought to be life satisfaction. (When he rotated this factor plus a few factors of minor importance, he found three of the factors to be similar to three of the postulated components--Mood Tone, Zest for Life, and Congruence between Desired and Achieved Goals.)

Wilker (1975) submitted ten of the original Life Satisfaction Index A items to a factor analysis. The items were included in a survey of a sample of New York City residents living in Inner City neighborhoods characterized by poverty, decay and social disorganization. He reported three factors-- Dissatisfaction with Present Life; Satisfaction with Present Life; and Overall Evaluation of Past Life--which correspond roughly to the components of Mood tone, Zest, and Resolution/Fortitude in the original scale. He also found that the three factors were differentially related to such variables as social participation, income, worries, and the like. Wilker's analysis thus underscores the multidimensionality of the Life Satisfaction Index.

Recent efforts have more methodically aimed at the development of multidimensional scales and have utilized samples of older people. A pool of 45 items from several sources thought to be related to morale were included in a large study with elderly people from the community and from a psychiatric hospital ward (Pierce and Clark, 1973). A cluster analysis identified three morale-related clusters, namely Depression/Satisfaction, Equanimity, and Will to Live. These three factors distinguished between hospitalized and community respondents, with the community residents demonstrating more satisfaction, more equanimity and greater will to live. (The remaining three clusters appeared to be related to attitudes towards aging, to social accessibility, and to physical health.)

Another widely used scale is the Philadelphia Geriatric Center Morale Scale. The 22 item-scale was originally developed by Lawton (1972) and subsequently employed on different samples and factor-analyzed by Lawton

(1972, 1975), and by Morris and Sherwood (1975). Three factors have been reproduced consistently in these studies--Agitation; Attitude toward Aging; and Lonely Dissatisfaction.

Lawton (1977) completed a comprehensive review of all the existing measures of subjective well-being and identified several dimensions which emerge as relatively independent in different investigations using various item pools and populations. These are (1) positive intrapsychic states (i.e., happiness, life satisfaction, mood, positive self-concept); (2) intra-psychic symptoms (i.e., anxiety, depression); (3) morale-related aspects of psychophysiological and somatic symptoms (i.e., headaches, tiredness, loss of appetite); (4) interactive states (i.e., anomie, loneliness); and (5) self-rated health. Among those dimensions the "positive intrapsychic states" represent the core of the concept as most students of aging would define it.

We tend to agree with George and Bearon (1980) that for the sake of clarity, the concept is better restricted to "intrapsychic states." The inclusion of other factors such as self-perceived health, social interactions, and the like, make the concept theoretically less useful. As Carp (1977) and Sherwood (1977) have pointed out, this is due to the confounding of some of the most frequently researched determinants of subjective well-being--health and social interactions--with dimensions of the concept itself, resulting in inflated relationships between potential determinants and the concept. Thus, since subjective well-being is often viewed as the outcome of long-term socialization and developmental processes as well as concurrent environmental conditions, such a confounding is most unfortunate for testing the various theories.

Several conceptualizations of intrapsychic states have been proposed. Among them, Bradburn (1969) developed a measure of "mental health" that could be used with a general non-clinical population. Using a set of ten items measuring affective states with a sample of American adults from several cities, he found two dimensions--positive and negative affect--that were independent of each other. Each dimension by itself as well as the difference between them was related to self-reported happiness and thus seemed to tap a similar concept. On the other hand, the two dimensions were differentially related to various postulated correlates: anxiety and physical symptoms were related to the negative but not to the positive affect dimension, while social participation was related to the positive but not to the negative affect dimension. Such differential correlations tend to underscore the independence of the identified dimensions. As discussed before, the structure of a positive and a negative affect dimension was replicated by Wilker (1975) on a sample of older residents using items from the Life Satisfaction Index A of Neugarten et al. (1961). Wilker also reported similar differential relationships to postulated correlates. On the basis of his results, Bradburn argued that subjective well-being is composed of independent positive and negative components. In other words, a person may be having some good feelings and at the same time some bad feelings about some parts of his or her life. Consequently, he labeled his measure of subjective well-being the "affect balance scale."

Working also from a social indicator perspective, Campbell et al. (1976) and Andrews and Withey (1976) proposed still another conceptualization of subjective well-being. They viewed the intrapsychic states as a composite of satisfactions with the major domains of life such as marriage, job, leisure, family, and housing. This research tended to show that satisfactions experienced in a set of about ten to fifteen major domains of life account for approximately half of the variance in overall satisfaction with life.[1] If the domain satisfactions are submitted to some form of structural analysis (e.g., cluster analysis or factor analysis), several rather distinctive dimensions appear. While the exact form of the configuration depends, of course, on the set of items which are included in the analysis, the areas of marriage and family, of work, of leisure, of friends and other people in general, of the economic situation, of housing and community, of health, of organizations, and of self can usually be distinguished as relatively separate aspects.

In sum, even conceptualizations of subjective well-being as intrapsychic states and relevant measures differ on several accounts. Thus, life satisfaction, happiness, or "affect balance" refer to the entire life, while satisfaction with housing, work, family, and the like, refer to specific domains of life. Or, some concepts such as satisfaction implicitly refer to a much more extended time span than happiness or affect balance. Also, as Andrews and Withey (1976) have pointed out, satisfaction ratings are somewhat more influenced by cognitive processes whereby the person compares their current state of affairs to some desired state of affairs. This is in contrast to the happiness measures which appear to be more emotionally based.

Explanations of subjective well-being

A large part of gerontological work has dealt with the explanation of subjective well-being. (A recent comprehensive review is provided by Larson, 1978.) Two major theoretical positions focus on activities and roles of older people as an indication of their involvement in the world around them. One of the theoretical positions is disengagement theory, originally formulated by Cumming and Henry in 1961. It maintains that successful aging as reflected in high life satisfaction is related to a withdrawal from social activities and interactions. In other words, the old person who "retires" from an active engagement in his or her social world will be the one who retains high satisfaction with life and ages successfully. However, disengagement theory

---

[1] Of course, part of the relationship between domain satisfactions and overall subjective well-being observed in these studies is attributable to similarity of the response scales; i.e., an identical scale of satisfaction was used to measure satisfaction with each domain as well as overall well-being, and respondents tended to use a particular scale in similar ways irrespective of the content that was being measured. This issue has recently received more systematic attention by Andrews and Crandall (1976) who developed a data matrix and analysis procedure that enable them to distinguish the contribution of method factors to the level of interrelationships among satisfaction variables from the contribution of content factors, and they report that a substantial amount of the interrelationships can be attributed to method similarity. In other words, the overall interrelationships between satisfaction variables is at least partly due to the identical response scales that are being used to measure the various satisfactions.

has not been confirmed by a number of studies which have tested its basic propositions. (For reviews see Botwinick, 1973; Maddox, 1970; Neugarten, 1973.) Most empirical evidence supports instead an alternative theoretical position--activity theory. According to this theoretical position, the older person who remains active and retains frequent interactions with his or her social world ages more successfully than the person who experiences a shrinkage of his social world (Havighurst et al., 1968). Activity theory thus maintains that a decrease in social interaction which is undoubtedly associated with older age results from a withdrawal by society from the older person but takes place largely against the wishes of most older people (Havighurst et al., 1968). Most likely, both positions reflect part of the truth: while many older people will be happier with higher levels of activities, a few will actually be happier with lower levels of activities (Maddox, 1965; Maddox and Wiley, 1976).

Another theoretical framework focuses on the significance of <u>resources</u> such as income, education, health, or marital status in producing subjective well-being. High income, good health, and the presence of a spouse are assumed not only to be enjoyed in themselves, but also to provide the means that can facilitate other types of enjoyment. For example, older people who are in better health and have more financial means can engage in more activities, which in turn are likely to improve their morale, as discussed above (Bull and Aucoin, 1975; Cutler, 1973). Resource factors are quite consistently found to relate positively to subjective well-being among the aged (Edwards and Klemmack, 1973; George, 1978; Maddox and Eisdorfer, 1962; Palmore and Luikart, 1972; Spreitzer and Snyder, 1974) as well as among the general population (Andrews and Withey, 1976, Campbell et al., 1976; Wilson, 1967), although in neither case are the effects very strong.

Finally, a set of factors that have been examined frequently for their potential effect but with a somewhat less clear rationale than the previous sets has been found to relate less consistently to subjective well-being. These variables refer to a variety of <u>sociodemographic factors</u> such as sex and race. Although not as clearly resources as the previous set of factors, these factors may be viewed as stratification variables which signify differential access to the resources of this society. And, of course, sex and race differentials in income, authority in the work place, or position in the political power structure have been amply documented.

As indicated by the foregoing discussion, many of the proposed predictors of subjective well-being are related to each other and thus may account for overlapping parts of the variance. A methodological implication of the interrelationships between predictors is that they need to be investigated within a multivariate analysis procedure.

A criticism which must be leveled at most of these theoretical positions is that they consider only the significance of the quantitative and objective aspects of various activities and resources (i.e., level of income; number of friends; etc.) but do not take into account the quality and subjective aspects of many of those factors. For example, the absolute level of income may be less critical than the level of satisfaction with it. Or the number of visits with family may be less important than the satisfaction with relationships with family. (Lowenthal and Robinson, 1976, and Conner, Powers, and Bultena, 1979, have raised a similar point.)

Moreover, it has been suggested repeatedly that an assessment of subjective well-being in older age must include the perspectives of older people themselves (Bloom, 1977; Carp, 1977), a view which has not remained uncontested, since some may question the respondents' competence to explain their own actions (Taylor, 1977).

Life span patterns of explanations of subjective well-being

While early gerontological research had focused exclusively on aged individuals, increasing recognition is being given to a life-span orientation, according to which morale in older age is viewed as a result of life-long developments. Thus, morale reported in older age is in some systematic way related to previous morale. In other words, we would expect a certain continuity or regularity of the patterns of morale across the life span. It also suggests that effects of current factors such as income level or employment status cannot necessarily be conceptualized as identical for different age levels because of potential interactions with previous experiences that individuals at different age levels may have experienced.

Some theoretical conceptualizations of life cycle patterns have clear implications for the study of development and change of subjective well-being across the life span. Among them, Rosow (1976) describes the age patterns of major roles and related activities, adopting a position similar to that of activity theory which views involvement in society and its institutions as promoting high morale. In particular, he describes a rather sharp increase and subsequent decrease in what he calls "institutional" roles across the life span. These institutional roles include, among others, major work and family roles. In contrast, he postulates a much flatter life cycle curve for informal roles indicating that less change occurs in these particular roles as the individual progresses through life. Informal roles include those of friend, informal leader, etc., all of which are usually assumed to have some bearing on subjective well-being. In contrast to the other two types of roles, a U-shaped relationship is postulated for what Rosow terms the "tenuous" roles, which are essentially empty or vague. In sum, he observes that older people—as well as very young people—occupy altogether fewer roles than middle-aged people, and that in particular they occupy less frequently those roles which are of major social significance.

Some authors view this attrition of the world of older adults as welcome relaxation from demands and responsibilities at a time in their lives when health problems often prohibit intensive involvement. However, social involvements represent something more than merely burdens. Social roles also have the important function of providing normative guidelines for appropriate behaviors and expectations; and thus they help the individual to integrate himself or herself into society and provide him or her with a sense of serving a useful function (Rosow, 1973). And when social functions are properly fulfilled, this usually results in a sense of personal satisfaction for the individual as well as in social recognition from others. Viewed in this latter way, the shrinkage of their world makes adjustment to older age difficult for the elderly because it remains largely unclear which interests and behaviors are appropriate for older persons and from where they should draw their satisfaction and a sense of happiness (Rosow, 1976). Briefly, this society provides few indications to older people on how to acquire happiness and satisfaction once they have completed their major societal tasks of worker and parent.

The challenge for older adults then becomes primarily one of identifying possible alternative sources of satisfaction by engaging in new roles and tasks (Friedman and Havighurst, 1954) or by expanding and consolidating existing ones (Atchley, 1972). Mentioned as possible alternatives have been the leisure role (Friedman and Havighurst, 1959; Streib and Schneider, 1971), the volunteer role (Streib and Schneider, 1971), and the citizen role (Streib and Schneider, 1971). While it is, however, quite obvious that some alternatives to losses of interpersonal and work roles may be available, replacements become increasingly more difficult to attain as a person ages. Examples are the loss of spouse, life-long friend, or work, which are often not replaceable.

Resources--another major set of predictors of subjective well-being-- generally also show a decline in older age. The foremost example is health. Among people over 65 more than 40 percent report limitations in activities due to health or physical condition compared to somewhat over 10 percent in the total population (U.S. Department of HEW, 1979) and about 85 percent report at least one chronic disease (Shanas and Maddox, 1976). Another fairly obvious example of a loss in resources is the reduction in income after retirement. Although income increases within the younger age groups, an aggregate decrease sets in after age 55 (U.S. Bureau of the Census, 1976). Adjustment for family size is likely to mitigate the effect somewhat, since older people have smaller families to support; but the fact remains that people over 65 are still overrepresented among the population in poverty (U.S. Bureau of the Census, 1979).

In the above discussion, two different types of change (or difference) have been alluded to which need to be differentiated more clearly now. Most of the discussion dealt with declines in various resources and interpersonal relationships with age and with the hypothesis that such declines might be related to a parallel decline in subjective well-being. Such age differences refer to differences in means, a focus which is very different from the issue of age differences in strength of relationships between roles/relationships and well-being. In the latter case, the focus is on differences in relationships rather than in means. Consider the following example. It has been reported that health has a much stronger impact on well-being in older age than in other age groups while the impact of income seems to be similar for all age levels (Spreitzer and Snyder, 1974). At the same time, health as well as income declines with increasing age. In other words, differences in average levels of resources such as income or health are only consequential for well-being to the extent that they retain their predictive importance at different age levels. Put somewhat differently, by means of this differentiation it might be possible to identify a mechanism by which morale could be maintained into old age: as some resources decline when people get older, older people may shift the sources of their feelings of well-being and thereby avoid experiencing an overall decline in well-being. Concretely, an older woman who has lost her spouse may turn to her friends or her children as an alternative source of psychological well-being.

Data used in our investigations

     Our investigations are entirely based on secondary analysis of data that were previously collected. A number of large national studies exist that can be brought to bear on the issues of interest. Unlike data used in many of the earlier studies, these data sets offer the following advantages: sampling procedures that allow--within specified error margins--generalization to the total United States population; carefully developed question wording and questionnaire construction; and data collection carried out with close attention to the field work. We consider the studies that we chose of high quality and an excellent means for a cost-effective investigation of the issues of interest.

     The specific studies examined in this report include: the set of social indicator studies conducted in 1972 by Andrews and Withey; a combined set of the seven General Social Surveys conducted annually from 1972 through 1978 by the National Opinion Research Center (Davis et al., 1978)[2]; a combined set of three Omnibus surveys conducted by the Survey Research Center between 1973 and 1975; an Omnibus survey conducted by the Survey Research Center in 1976; a social indicator study of the Detroit area (Rodgers et al., 1975); the 1976 replication of "Americans View their Mental Health" by Veroff, Douvan, and Kulka; and the Quality of Life survey conducted by Campbell et al. in 1971 as well as its replication conducted by Campbell and Converse in 1978.[3] With the exception of the two earliest General Social Surveys and the Detroit Social Indicator Study, all of these studies used full probability samples of American adults living in private households.[4] Sample size varied in size from 1,100 to to approximately 10,000. Thus, for the most part the respondents can be considered representative of the American non-institutionalized population.[5]

     Since the samples of these studies are multistage, stratified cluster samples rather than simple random samples, traditional tests of significance may not be accurate. This is the case because the selected households are clustered (typically about four households are selected from a small geographic area such as a city block) and therefore the estimates based on these samples have a larger error margin than if each household were selected independently. This loss in precision is taken into account in Chapters 3, 4, and 7 by using an "effective" number of respondents for calculations of

---

[2] The seven surveys were used in pooled form, since several of the patterns that we first investigated separately by year of data collection were similar across years.

[3] About 20 percent of the respondents in the 1978 Quality of Life Survey were reinterviews from the 1971 survey.

[4] The two earliest General Social Surveys used probability sampling down to the block level, quota sampling on the block level; the Detroit Social Indicator Study used a probability sample of the Detroit metropolitan area.

[5] Several of these data sets are archived by the Inter-University Consortium for Social and Political Research.

significance levels that is two thirds of the actual sample size.[*]

All of the studies that we used contain a set of subjective well-being
measures. A few of those measures refer to global feelings of satisfaction or
happiness, but most of them assess satisfaction with particular domains of
life. While the domains are similar across studies, they are not always
phrased in the same way. For example, some questions probe "family life,"
while others ask about "things you do with your family"; or some refer to
"spare" time, others to "leisure" time. Most of the studies use seven-point
scales to measure satisfaction, but the nomenclature differs from study to
study. Respondents in the Quality of Life and the Detroit Social Indicator
studies could give answers ranging from "Completely satisfied" to "Completely
dissatisfied"; in the General Social Survey the extreme alternatives were "A
very great deal (of satisfaction)" and "None"; in the Social Indicator studies
and 1973-1975 Omnibus surveys respondents were offered a series of choices
ranging from "Delighted" to "Terrible"; and finally, the 1976 Omnibus survey
used a split-ballot technique according to which a random half of the sample
responded with a "Delighted-Terrible" scale, while the other half used the
"Completely satisfied-Completely dissatisfied" response scale. A few
miscellaneous scales were used for single items, one item in particular,
probing present happiness, was included in six of the seven studies; three
response alternatives were given: "Very happy," "Pretty happy," and "Not too
happy." In the General Social Surveys marriage satisfaction was measured by a
question asking about happiness in marriage and providing the above 3-point
scale, satisfaction with finances was measured by a 3-point and satisfaction
with work by a 4-point response scale. For the complete questions refer to
Appendix A.

A priori no conceptual distinctions between measures of happiness and
satisfaction and between different response scales are postulated. Despite
the differences in time frame or phrasing, the various measures tend to be
quite highly correlated (Andrews and Withey, 1976; Campbell et al., 1976), and
all are generally used as measures of the underlying concept of subjective
well-being (Larson, 1978). The final verdict on whether this assumption is
justified depends on the results of the analyses to be reported below.

Wherever possible, we repeated the same analysis with several data sets.
Although the measures of subjective well-being are not worded in exactly the
same form in the different data sets, the replication of a finding is
particularly impressive when it appears independent of the specifics of the
question wording.

Organization of this volume

In Chapter 2 and Chapter 3 we address the issue of age differences in
meaning systems of subjective well-being. We first examine people's responses
to open-ended questions asking them about what makes them happy, unhappy, and

---

[*] We assume that the design effect has a typical value of 1.5, which is
consistent with values actually calculated for design effects of samples and
variables of the type discussed here.

worried, in an effort to determine if similar meaning systems emerge across various age groups. We also perform factor analyses of measures of satisfaction with various life domains in order to determine whether the structure of satisfactions is similar across age groups.

In Chapter 4 we examine the relationship between age and a number of measures of the various dimensions of subjective well-being. By replicating our analysis across seven data sets we hope to more firmly establish the exact nature of the relationship between age and satisfaction. We also examine the usefulness of some of the various explanations of this relationship put forward in the literature.

In Chapter 5 we examine the relationship between a series of demographic variables such as sex, race, income, marital status, etc. and overall subjective well-being. We ask whether a similar set of demographic characteristics explain subjective well-being and whether the relationships are similar in magnitude and direction across the various age groups.

In Chapter 6 we similarly examine the relationship between satisfaction with various domains of life and overall subjective well-being. Major attention is focused on determining whether satisfaction with these various domains contribute to overall subjective well-being in similar ways among various age groups.

In Chapter 7 we look at the effect of working vs. being retired on subjective well-being among older people. We also look at what role various patterns of activities play in helping or hindering successful adjustment to retirement.

CHAPTER 2

PERCEIVED SOURCES OF SUBJECTIVE WELL-BEING

This chapter examines sources of happiness, as they are described by the respondents themselves. As we maintained in the introduction, the perception of the respondents themselves are an important part of a concept so eminently subjective in nature as happiness or satisfaction. We believe that the views of the respondents need to set the stage for any investigation into the nature of subjective well-being and its patterns across the life span.

The data that are available to us refer to a set of open-ended questions asking about "what kinds of things" people worry about, what they are happy about, and what they are unhappy about. The questions were included in the beginning of the interview that was conducted by Veroff, Douvan, and Kulka in 1976 with a representative sample of the American population as a replication of the "American View their Mental Health" study conducted in 1957 (Veroff, Douvan, and Kulka, 1976).

Method

In particular, three questions are used that ask the respondent what makes him or her happy, unhappy, and worried, while leaving the formulation of the response entirely up to the respondent. For example, the exact formulation of the question about worrying was as follows: "Everyone has some things he worries about more or less. What kinds of things do you worry about most?"[7]

Responses to these open-ended questions are reported in the form of percentages of respondents who mentioned a particular category, by 10-year age brackets (Tables 2-1 through 2-3). Very detailed codes had been developed for the 1957 study and had been essentially retained for the 1976 study. For the present analysis summary codes were formed on the basis of the response patterns by age, such that major age patterns were preserved. Statistical significance of age differences in mentioning each category is evaluated by contingency table analysis. Since the X^2-values, as reported in the last column of each table, only provide estimates of the overall deviations of each cell frequencies from the marginal frequencies, but provide no indication as to which particular age level(s) account(s) for the relationship, age groups which show significantly higher or lower frequencies in a particular category than the average are marked with an asterisk. The identification of such deviant age levels is based on the Lambda values resulting from contingency

---

[7] The full text of the questions is given in Appendix A.

table analysis as proposed by Goodman (1972).

Findings

Sources of happiness

Let us first consider the reasons which older respondents (60 years old and older) mention for their happiness. The results in Table 2-1 are quite clear; today's older citizens report predominantly three sources of happiness, each of which are mentioned by about one quarter of all the older respondents. These sources are their economic situation, their health, and the relationship they maintain with their children. The predominance of these mentions suggests that a comfortable economic situation, enjoyable relations with one's children, and no worries about health figure highly when older respondents evaluate their happiness. On the other hand, several sources which are often cited by students of aging as particularly critical in providing a sense of subjective well-being at a time of attrition of life space are mentioned only infrequently: the contacts older persons maintain with people other than their relatives, the activities and hobbies they engage in, and the independence they enjoy in their personal situation are mentioned by only 5 to 10 percent; relationships with spouse are mentioned even less frequently.

Consider next the pattern of reported sources of happiness across the life course. In examining the frequency of mentions of any source, we will be particularly interested in systematic patterns across age levels, which would suggest age-related shifts. Among the three sources which are most frequently cited by the aged respondents as discussed above, different patterns emerge among other age groups. While happiness about economic means is mentioned about equally by all age groups, and thus does not lend itself to an age-related interpretation, health as a source of happiness clearly does so. Mentions of health show the strongest age-related pattern in Table 2-1. Mentions of this particular source are much higher among the aged than among younger age groups and exhibit a rather linear increase across age levels. Older people appear to be clearly more appreciative of good health than younger people. This--we presume--is based on older people's increased anticipation of health problems and on their recognition that good health at their age is not guaranteed; in other words, we believe that the finding reflects a life course phenomenon.

Frequency of mentioning children as a source of happiness reflects another likely life cycle phenomenon. Although mentioned frequently by every age group, younger and middle-aged respondents (30-39 and 40-49 year olds) are even more likely to mention this source. In these age groups respondents are also most likely to have children at home and to experience them as a major focus of their lives, whereas in other age groups many children are not yet born or have already left home.

Several sources of happiness decline in frequency of mentions across age levels and thus appear of minor importance among the older respondents, as discussed above. Among them, work and education are mentioned with decreasing frequency as age increases. The marital relationship is also mentioned less frequently among older respondents. These declines partly reflect the decreasing percentages of respondents who are actually married, working, or going to school. But while among working respondents mentioning of job and among married respondents mentioning of marriage indeed do not decline as sharply (data not shown), the general tendency persists. In other words, older respondents are somewhat less inclined to mention the roles of worker and spouse, even if they still occupy the particular role, and are probably shifting their attention to other sources of happiness. What are then some of the likely sources for happiness among older respondents?

Among the variables which are traditionally considered as critical in adjusting to old age and in dealing with the shrinking life space, only activities and hobbies are mentioned more frequently by the 60 to 69 year olds than by the total sample. This latter finding provides some evidence that activities and hobbies may become more important for the relatively young respondents among the old who have fewer commitments than young and middle-aged groups but still enough energy to pursue a variety of leisure activities. Interestingly, the age group who mentions activities and hobbies least frequently and significantly less than the average are respondents between 40 and 49 years of age. We suspect that this latter finding is due to the fact that responsibilities and commitments--i.e., work, marriage, and family--are probably highest in this particular age group, and happiness is based on successful handling of those commitments rather than on satisfying activities and hobbies.

Sources of unhappiness

In accord with sources cited for happiness, present health and economic situation are also frequently mentioned as reasons for unhappiness by aged respondents (i.e., about 15 to 20 percent mention each source) (Table 2-2). This finding suggests that the same domains which are perceived as sources of happiness when fulfilled are perceived as sources of unhappiness when not fulfilled. Major exceptions to this rule are relations with own children, which are often mentioned as a source of happiness but not of unhappiness, and social, political, and moral issues, which emerge frequently as sources of unhappiness but not of happiness. Although we do not have a ready explanation for this exception, we believe that it may reflect a form of dealing with upsetting and threatening questions by displacing answers into a less personal realm--i.e., social problems--away from the very personal realm of one's children and their problems. Alternatively, lack of mentioning family as sources of unhappiness may reflect a social desirability effect, since it is not generally acceptable to be unhappy about one's family.

Once again, the age trajectories of sources of unhappiness differ considerably. The strongest and approximately linear increase is observed for mentioning of health-related concerns; these may be one's own or spouse's health problems. A less strong but still statistically significant increase with age is observed for the mentioning of the actual lack of a spouse. Note, however, that older respondents are less likely to mention problems in their marital relationship as a source for unhappiness than are middle-aged and younger respondents, a relationship which parallels the declining frequency of mentioning the marital relationship as a reason for happiness. However, in this case the decrease in mentions is not statistically significant if only the married respondents are examined (data not shown).

Reasonably clear age declines are also found in mentions of economic and job-related concerns. While the decline in mentioning jobs is consistent with the reasons cited for happiness (and persists when only job holders are considered), the decline in economic sources of unhappiness is more puzzling in light of the rather limited financial means of many aged individuals. It may, however, be the case that older persons are less dependent on economic means for their subjective well-being, since as means decline, so do financial needs, responsibilities and, perhaps most important, financial uncertainty. Alternatively, older people may simply be less willing to admit to unhappiness about their economic status.

Mentions of children, their problems, and the contacts with them--though much less frequently cited overall--show an age trend similar to mentions of children as a source of happiness, i.e., the percentages are significantly higher among middle-aged respondents than among older and younger respondents.

Whereas the findings thus far do not indicate any area of increased significance in creating unhappiness for the aged, the frequencies observed for mentioning non-relatives carry such a connotation. Both the older and the younger age groups cite this source more often than the middle-aged group. Concretely, this implies that the malfunction of friendships is a more salient reason for unhappiness among the aged and the young than among other age groups, implying perhaps the increased importance of friendships in these two age groups and the lack of family as an alternative source.

Sources of worries

In response to the question of what they worry about (Table 2-3), a question which appears to have more of a future orientation to it than the question about reasons for unhappiness, the most frequent responses of the older respondents are nevertheless quite similar to those given to the question about unhappiness. Worries about present economic and health situation lead the field; worries about future health and economic problems are less prevalent but still sizeable. Worries about social issues are also mentioned quite frequently.

Moreover, age patterns of the reasons for worrying are similar to those for unhappiness. Specifically, worries about health increase, worries about economic situation and job decrease, and worries about children show an inverted U-shaped relationship. Also note the age-related increase in respondents who say that they never worry.

Summary and Discussion

When older adults consider their happiness, unhappiness, and worries, they talk about some similar sources as younger people. For example, their

17

economic situation seems critical to them for subjective well-being. Or their
children seem to them to play a major role in their happiness. Or societal
issues seem to worry them.

At the same time, several domains of life which are quite salient to
younger adults appear of little importance to older adults in assessing their
subjective well-being. Such include the world of work, educational endeavors,
and the marital relationship. To a considerable degree this decline in the
subjective salience of those domains reflects the decline in prevalence of the
student, worker, and spouse roles as people get older; fewer older people are
in school or at work, or have a living spouse, than young or even middle-aged
respondents. Interestingly, however, these differences in role occupancy do
not explain the entire effect. If work-related mentions are examined only
among respondents who are actually in the work force or if mentions of the
marital relationship are examined only among married respondents,
relationships with age are less strong but the trend nevertheless persists.
We believe that this "tuning out" by older people who still occupy those roles
is created by their anticipation of relinquishing the particular role and an
attempt to loosen their reliance on it in preparation for the change. De-
emphasis of the worker and the marital role as observed in these data may well
be part of preparation for that transition.

Given that older respondents do not perceive these major roles of adult
life as important for their subjective well-being as do other adults, which
aspects of human existence do they believe to be critical? As noted before,
economic means and children are mentioned frequently by older adults as
constituting sources of subjective well-being for them. Health is also
mentioned frequently by this age group, and reflects a strong increase
compared to younger adults. On a closer look at least two of these sources do
not, however, appear as alternatives to lost work and marital roles since they
refer also to a potential loss. Older respondents are much more likely to
mention health as an important source, since--if they do not already have
health problems--they are certainly aware that good health is not guaranteed
at their age. Thus, it is most likely the actual or potential loss of good
health which raises the saliency of this resource for older people. A similar
case may be made with respect to economic resources. That this particular
resource is perceived as critical throughout the life cycle may well have to
do with the persistent possibility of its being threatened.

Relationships with their children is the major interpersonal source of
happiness that older respondents mention with high frequency. At the same
time they almost never implicate this relationship as creating unhappiness or
worries. Despite this relatively high frequency of mentions, the results also
indicate a relative decline in importance of the parental role compared to the
middle years, since middle-aged respondents mention children even more
frequently as a source of happiness as well as a source of worries and
unhappiness. Still, children are seen as playing a major role in providing
happiness for older people, while not creating a comparable level of worries
and unhappiness.

We are then still left with the question of whether there are any aspects
of human existence which are viewed as sources of well-being with increasing
frequency by older adults and therefore may represent potential substitutes
for the losses encountered in other areas of life. From the results presented

thus far, hobbies and activities, as well as the relationships with non-relatives, appear to assume this function to some degree, although the absolute level of response frequencies does not single them out as particularly salient contributors to subjective well-being.

It is also interesting to note that the factors which are cited by the respondents as contributing to their happiness are fairly similar to the factors seen as contributing to their unhappiness and worries. This suggests that positive and negative emotions may not be different in what people view as their causes, and lends some support to the notion that positive and negative affects are the two poles of the same dimension, as opposed to the notion of relatively independent positive and negative dimensions of subjective well-being as proposed by Bradburn (1969).

Table 2-1

Percentage of Respondents Mentioning Each
Source as Reason for Happiness, by Age

Age:	Total	20-29	30-39	40-49	50-59	60-69	70-79	80++	Chi-square
Reason:									
Spouse									
Spouse's situation	1	0	1	1	3*	1	2	0	14.98*
Respondent's relationship w. spouse	17	24*	20*	21*	16	11	4*	4*	79.39**
Children									
Children's situation	2	3	3	4*	1	1	1	4	15.47*
Respondent's relationship w. children	27	22*	31*	35*	29	22	22	23	29.68**
Other Relatives									
Other relatives' situation	0	0	0	1*	0	0	1	0	9.19
Respondent's relationship w. other relatives	3	3	1*	3	4	3	4	5	12.84*
Non-relatives									
Respondent's relationship w. non-relatives	8	14*	8	4*	2*	7	9	9	49.21**
Health									
Respondent's present health	12	3*	5*	8*	17*	24*	21*	29*	148.77**
Economic Situation									
Respondent's present material resources	28	24*	27	29	30	31	30	25	7.82
Work Situation									
Respondent's job	17	23*	23*	17*	16	9	3	0	105.73**
Personal Situation									
Respondent's activities, hobbies	6	7	5	3*	4	9*	9	6	16.78*
Respondent's independence	7	11*	7	3*	5	5	7	5	23.73**
Respondent's education	3	8*	3	4	1	1	1	0	53.34**
Other	4	4	4	4	5	2	5	1	7.82
Happy about everything	5	4	6	8	3*	7	6	6	13.27*

Note: Up to 3 mentions were coded; therefore the percentages add up to more than 100%.

Table 2-2

Percentage of Respondents Mentioning Each
Source as Reason for Unhappiness, by Age

Age:	Total	20-29	30-39	40-49	50-59	60-69	70-79	80++	Chi-square
Reason:									
Spouse									
Spouse, general	1	1	2	1	1	0	1*	0	4.19
Lack of spouse	3	1	3	3	2	5	8*	0	27.15**
Spouse's situation	2	1	2	2	3	2	4*	0	14.33*
Respondent's relationship w. spouse	4	5*	5	4	3	2	1	0	19.40**
Children									
Children, general	1	1	2	2	1	1	1	0	7.49
Lack of children	1	1	1	0	0	1	2	1	11.88
Children's situation	3	1*	3	7*	5*	5	2	3	35.33**
Respondent's relationships w. children	4	3	4	4	6*	3	6*	1	12.15
Other Relatives									
Other relatives' situation	6	9*	7	4	4	5	7	4	16.47*
Non-relatives									
Respondent's relationship w. non-relatives	7	10*	4	3*	5	9	10*	6	29.54**
Health									
Respondent's present health	8	4*	4*	7*	9	12	17*	32*	88.50**
Respondent's future health	1	0	1	0	1	2	3	5*	21.23**
Economic Situation									
Respondent's present material resources	21	29*	24*	20	14*	14*	16	15	48.82**
Respondent's future material resources	1	1	1	1	0	1	2	1	2.92
Other econ. unhappiness	2	4	2	1	2	3	2	0	9.92
Work Situation									
Respondent's job	19	29*	25*	21*	16*	9	2*	4*	138.79**
Personal Situation									
Respondent's independence	0	1*	0	0	0	0	0	0	14.25*
Respondent's achievements	5	5	7*	5	6	4	1	0	19.19**
Spiritual	1	1*	1	1	0	0	0	0	9.41
Personal situation, general	3	3	4	2	3	2	3	3	2.57
Societal Concerns									
Crime	2	1	2	2	3	3	2	3	7.98
Morality	7	5	6	8	7	9	8	10	6.74
Economy/Politics	20	16	21	26*	22	20	19	14	14.83*
Other									
Other	1	1	1	1	1	1	2	0	3.25
General unhappiness	2	3	2	2	2	3	1	5	5.49

Note: Up to 3 mentions were coded; therefore the percentages add up to more than 100%.

Table 2-3

Percentage of Respondents Mentioning Each
Source as Reason for Worries, by Age

Age:	Total	20-29	30-39	40-49	50-59	60-69	70-79	80++	Chi-square
Reason:									
Spouse									
Spouse, general	1	1	1	1	1	0	0*	0	7.90
Lack of spouse	1	1	1	0	0	0	3*	0	11.59
Spouse's situation	4	2*	3	3	7*	7*	6	3	22.17**
Respondent's relationship w. spouse	1	2	3*	1	0	0	1	0	15.40*
Children									
Children, general	12	8	16*	18*	15*	7	7	4	47.18**
Children's situation	8	7	9	12*	10*	5	4*	6	22.36**
Respondent's relationship w. children	5	5	10*	7*	4	0	2	1	60.62**
Other Relatives									
Other relatives' situation	11	8	11	16*	12	13	9	8	15.53*
Other Relatives									
Non-relatives situation	0	0	0*	0	0	0	0	3	7.75
Respondent's relationship w. non-relatives	3	3	4*	1	1	2	5*	1	22.54**
Health									
Health, general	3	2*	3	4	6*	3	4	3	12.18
Respondent's present health	8	3*	3*	8	10	13*	21*	25*	106.36**
Respondent's future health	5*	3*	3*	3	6*	8*	10*	13	38.83**
Economic Situation									
Respondent's present material resources	32	45*	39*	31*	23	23	19*	10*	109.79**
Respondent's future material resources	5	5	4	6	6	5	2*	5	8.16
Other economic worries	2	3	1	1	1	2	2	0	8.65
Work Situation									
Respondent's job	15	25*	18*	14*	12	7	2*	4	106.54**
Personal Situation									
Personal situation, general	1*	3	1	0	0	1	1	0	19.13**
Respondent's achievements	2	3	4*	3	1	2	0	1	15.55**
Spiritual	1	1	0	1	0	0	1	1	7.90
Societal Concerns									
Crime	2	2	1	2	3	3	4	3	5.51
Morality	6	3	4	7	7	7	8	1	17.31**
Economy/Politics	16	13*	14	14	20	20	21	17	16.65*
Other									
Worry always	1	2	2	1	1	4	1	0	8.26
Worry	5	9*	5	4	4	4	4	3	0.00
Never worry	5	3*	3*	4	7	6	10*	24*	54.43**

Note: Up to 3 mentions were coded; therefore the percentages add up to more than 100%.

CHAPTER 3

STRUCTURE OF SUBJECTIVE WELL-BEING IN DIFFERENT AGE GROUPS*

Subjective well-being is frequently conceptualized as multi-dimensional (e.g., Adams, 1971; Campbell et al., 1976; Lawton, 1975; Neugarten et al., 1961). This multidimensionality requires investigating not only quantitative age differences, but also qualitative or structural age differences. The latter refer to the meaning and composition of the concept of well-being: any age differences found in the structural composition of subjective well-being would indicate that at different ages people hold different concepts of subjective well-being. Such qualitative investigations are particularly critical if quantitative comparisons of subjective well-being are to be made, since a concept with uniform meaning is essential for making comparisons of the level of subjective well-being across age groups (Baltes et al., 1977).

Studies by Campbell et al. (1976) and by Andrews and Withey (1976) have directed some attention to whether the structure of subjective well-being varies across age groups. Campbell et al. have reported that the distinct dimensions that can usually be identified as underlying satisfactions with the major life domains--marriage and family, work, leisure, friends and people in general, the economic situation, housing and community, health, organizations, and self--remain fairly similar across age levels. Andrews and Withey, while also stressing the similarity, noted that the interrelationships between dimensions (i.e., clusters in their particular form of analysis) showed some variation. We will return to this issue somewhat later.

Recently, Cutler (1979) has challenged the concept of a stable structure of subjective well-being across age levels and raised questions concerning the appropriateness of the concept for age comparisons. Specifically, he subjected 12 domains of life satisfaction from the Quality of Life study (Campbell et al., 1976) to factor analysis, performing a separate analysis with orthogonal factors for each age decade. Using a cut-off point of .5 for factor loadings, he displayed the resulting factors with the items which loaded at that level on any factor, and observed several irregularities in terms of the number of factors, the order in which they emerged, and the items which loaded on each factor. From these observations he concluded that the factor structure is rather dissimilar across age levels.

However, Cutler's (1979) analysis contains several shortcomings in that he failed to recognize several caveats raised by Cunningham (1978) regarding comparative factor analyses. Cunningham's caveats translate into the following recommendations for age comparisons in factor analyses.

1) Comparative factor analyses for separate age groups should be performed on the unstandardized variance-covariance matrices, because the metric must be the same for all age groups if differences are to be interpretable. At the very least, where correlation matrices are

---

*A slightly modified version of this chapter was previously published in _Journal of Gerontology_, 1981, 36, 472-479.

used, some evidence is needed to document that the variances by which correlation matrices were standardized are indeed similar across age groups.

2) Factor loading patterns should be compared across age groups only after they have been matched by means of rotation, since the orientation of the initial factor structure is completely arbitrary.

3) Careful attention needs to be given to the number of factors that are to be extracted; too few or too many factors may put undue strain on the data, with unpredictable results.

None of these three recommendations had been adopted by Cutler (1979) for his analysis. Looking back at the Campbell et al. analysis (1976), we note that while they did perform rotations, they did so on correlation matrices rather than on variance-covariance matrices, as Cunningham suggests.

At this point it may be useful to take a more general look at how differences in structure across age levels may express themselves. Taking a factor analytic approach, at least two different types of structural differences can be distinguished, as described in a recent theoretical paper by Alwin and Jackson (1980). First, the nature of the underlying dimensions or factors may be different, as would be evidenced if the specific measured variables loaded differently on the underlying factors. This type of structural difference is of central concern to investigations of factorial invariance, and we will refer to it here as difference in "factor loadings." Second, the underlying dimensions may have different variances or may interrelate in different ways; we will refer to this as difference in "factor relationships," recalling however that it includes differences in factor variances as well. The second form of structural differences is of course interpretable only if the dimensions are equal in the first place--that is, if the factor loadings of the measured variables are similar. Therefore the equality of the interrelationships between the factors should be tested only after having established the equality of the factors.

We applied these principles to the data previously analyzed by Cutler (1979) and by Campbell et al. (1976). We then repeated the analysis with another set of items, and with a different data set, obtaining in each analysis highly similar results which greatly enhances the confidence that can be put into the findings. In the following we will describe our analysis and point out how it differs from previous approaches.

Method

Data

The data reported in this chapter were collected as part of two national sample surveys of the adult population (age 18 and older) conducted in 1971 (N=2164) and 1978 (N=3692) (Campbell et al., 1976; Campbell, 1980). Both studies focused on measuring the subjective quality of life, and both asked a large number of questions about the respondent's satisfaction with life as a whole and with various specific life domains. The 1971 study contained two series of questions related to satisfactions with major domains of life; one series was repeated in the 1978 study. These three series of questions form the basis for our three sets of analyses.

Analytic procedures

The factor analyses reported in this paper were performed on variance-covariance matrices, unlike the analyses reported by Cutler (1979) and by Campbell et al. (1976) which were performed on correlation matrices. As noted above, Cunningham (1978) cautions against using correlation matrices for comparing factor structures, since the standardization on variances may obscure real differences that exist between the age groups. It should be noted that the issue here is not whether variables should be standardized to remove differences due to different scales. Standardization, if done separately for each age group and if those age groups have different variances on some or all of the variables, results effectively in variables with a different metric across age groups. This situation does not permit meaningful age comparisons. Specifically, for the set of questions used in Cutler's analysis, we find highly significant differences in variances across the seven age groups with the largest differences found in the item on "your health and physical condition": the variance on this item among those age 75 and older is almost three times as great as the variance among those age 18-24. Overall, seven of the twelve items have significantly different variances across the seven age levels, based on Bartlett's test for homogeneity of variance (p < .05; six of the twelve are different at the p < .01 level). Because of these differences in variances across age groups, the standardization implicit in correlation matrices produces variables that have different units in different age groups.

Another caution raised by Cunningham concerns the determination of the number of factors to be extracted and used for comparison of the age levels. Cutler used Kaiser's criterion to specify the number of factors needed for each age group, and although this is a commonly used criterion for factor analysis, it is quite arbitrary in a statistical sense, and can be misleading as a guide for comparing factor analyses from different groups. As an alternative, we obtained separate solutions to factor analyses for two, three, and four factors for each age group. Specifically, we used the Exploratory Factor Analysis Program (EFAP) developed by Joreskog and Sorbom (1976), which utilizes a maximum likelihood estimation procedure and provides a goodness-of-fit measure that is useful in evaluating the adequacy of a given number of factors. The goodness-of-fit statistic reflects the correspondence between the values generated by the hypothesized factor model and the values that are actually observed.

After determining the least number of factors that provided an adequate fit, we compared the different age groups by means of confirmatory factor analysis, using COFAMM (Confirmatory Factor Analysis with Model Modification, Sorbom and Joreskog, 1976). The reason for using confirmatory factor analysis and this particular program is that our primary objective was not so much to explore the nature of the structures of life satisfaction as it was to test the consistency of those structures across age groups and particularly to determine where the differences, if any, occur. COFAMM permits one to specify a hypothesis (or model) of equal loadings of the measured variables on the latent factors across age groups, which amounts to a test of equality of the nature of the factors. In doing this, COFAMM implicitly incorporates a process that can be thought of, in traditional factor analytic terminology, as the rotation of factor structures to maximize their congruence. The appropriateness of the specified model is evaluated by a goodness-of-fit statistic provided by COFAMM. If the fit of values predicted by this model is not significantly worse than the fit of values predicted by a model without constraints on the equality of factor loadings across age groups, the loadings could indeed be considered to be equal across age groups (with some unknown probability of making a Type II error).

If this model, with equal factor loadings for all age groups, provides an adequate fit to the observed values, the next step is to specify a model in which not only the loadings of the measured variables but also the relationships among the factors are to be equal across age levels. If the fit for such a hypothesis or model is not significantly different from the previous model (i.e., if the difference in the goodness-of-fit statistics is non-significant), then we can accept the hypothesis of equality of structure for the interrelationships among the dimensions as well as for the nature of the dimensions.

Findings

Repetition of Cutler's analysis: 12 variables and 7 age groups

Our first analysis involved twelve variables that measure the satisfaction derived from major life domains on a 7-point response scale ranging from "A very great deal" to "None." These variables were factor analyzed for each of seven age groups (essentially decades with minor variations). The variables and age groups are identical to those used by Cutler (1979).

The initial analysis determined the number of factors needed for subsequent analyses, using the EFAP program to obtain maximum likelihood solutions with two, three, and four factors for each of the seven age groups. The goodness-of-fit tests suggested that two factors are insufficient to describe the data for any of the age groups, and that three factors are sufficient to give an adequate fit for two of the age groups (age 25-34 and age 75 and older) but not for the remaining five groups (using a significance level of .05). Four factors, on the other hand, provided an adequate fit for all seven age groups, and consequently four factors are used in the subsequent analyses of these data.

The next step assessed the similarity of the loadings of the factors for the several age groups--that is, whether the relationship between the observed variables (i.e., satisfactions with specific domains) can be adequately explained in terms of a set of four underlying factors that are related in similar ways to the observed variables at all age levels.

According to our general strategy, (1) separate factor analyses were performed for the seven age groups, (2) a simultaneous factor analysis was performed for all seven age groups constraining the factor loadings to be equal across age groups, and (3) the goodness-of-fit statistic from the latter analysis was compared with the sum of the goodness-of-fit statistics from the seven separate analyses. (An added complexity is that it is necessary to specify k^2 constraints, where k is the number of factors, both for the separate analyses of the different age groups and for the combined analysis. These constraints are needed to identify the model, and in our experience various reasonable sets of constraints seem to provide similar goodness-of-fit statistics but produce differences with respect to the factor matrix and thus the interpretation of the meanings attached to the factors. The same constraints were used for all analyses of these data, and consisted of setting certain entries to 1 and others to 0.) The findings indicate that the model with equal factor pattern matrices in all age groups provides a poor fit to the data: the difference between the goodness-of-fit statistic for this model and the sum for the seven separate models is highly significant (X^2 = 272.2, df = 192, p = .0001). Examination of the residuals--the difference between the entries in the observed variance-covariance matrix for the twelve observed variables and the entries in the matrix predicted by the model--showed that the fit was worst for the youngest (18-24) and the oldest (75 and older) age groups. When the analysis was repeated for the five remaining age levels only, an adequate fit to the observed data was obtained. In conclusion, the four dimensions that underlie the 12 satisfaction measures seem similar for the five different age groups bracketed between the ages of 25 and 74.

The next step was to test the similarity of the relationships between the underlying factors across these five age levels. The adequacy of a model in which such constraints had been specified was tested by comparing its goodness-of-fit statistic with that for the previous model, without this constraint. The fit is significantly (p < .01) worse, suggesting that although the factors have similar meaning, they do not have similar variance and/or do not relate to each other in the same way.

In sum, our repetition of Cutler's analysis, modifying several features of the basic factor analytic procedure, led us to a conclusion that in some respects agrees and in some respects disagrees with his: we found some differences across age levels, but also some similarities. More specifically, the nature of the underlying factors is different for some age levels but not for all; major differences were observed for the very young (18-24) and the very old adults (75 and older). While the factor loadings appear to be similar across the 25-74 age range, their variances and interrelationships are significantly different even across age levels in this middle range.

Second analysis: New set of variables and 3 age groups

We turn now to another analysis, rather than dwelling on the results of the previous analysis, since aside from the strictly technical issues, we disagree with some other aspects of Cutler's analysis.

One area of disagreement is with Cutler's definition of age levels. Since the total sample consisted of fewer than 2,200 respondents, each of the seven individual age groups contains a rather small number of respondents, and resulting sample statistics are subject to considerable sampling error. (In particular the seventh age group in the previous analysis--those age 75 and older--consists of only approximately 100 respondents.) We therefore categorized the respondents into broader age groups, possibly losing some detail but increasing the confidence that can be placed in the findings for each age group. We also omitted those under age 25, on the assumption that young people are in the process of establishing their own independent lives and therefore may have less stable or "well-considered" structures of satisfaction; indeed, there was some suggestive evidence for this assumption in the first analysis.

Another area of disagreement is with Cutler's choice of the 12 variables from the Quality of Life study. As Campbell et al. (1976) had already pointed out, these 12 satisfaction measures were inferior to another set of variables that asked each respondent to describe himself or herself on a scale ranging from "Completely satisfied" to "Completely dissatisfied." Perhaps more important than differences in question wording or in the response scales is the fact that the 12 satisfaction items chosen by Cutler were asked as a set near the end of the interview, whereas the others were asked individually, each following a series of more specific questions about a particular domain. In this context, the respondent would have thought for a few minutes about a domain before summing up his or her satisfaction with it, and the responses may provide more reliable and valid information.

For our second analysis, we chose 11 domain satisfaction questions that were each asked in the context of a series of questions about the particular domain. The questions used a 7-point scale ranging from "Completely satisfied" to "Completely dissatisfied" and were also included in the 1971 Quality of Life survey. (Questions about the respondent's education, marriage, housework, and paid job, were omitted because they were not asked of all respondents.) For the reasons explained above, we defined three age groups: those 25-44, those 45-64, and those 65 or older. Analysis proceeded as before. The initial analysis, using EFAP, indicates that adequate fits may be obtained with three factors for the two younger age groups, but a questionable fit is observed for data from those age 65 and older (X^2=42.13, df=25, p=.017). Subsequent analyses were therefore performed with four factors.

The COFAMM program was used to compare the factor structures across the three age groups. The equivalence of the factor loadings across the three age groups was tested first. The goodness-of-fit statistic for a model that constrains the factor loadings to be equal for all three age groups is not significantly larger than that for a model that does not impose this constraint (X^2 = 71.69, df = 56, p = .077). We therefore do not reject the null hypothesis that the factor loadings are equal for the three age groups.

The estimated factor "loadings" for all three of these age groups are shown in Table 3-1. The first factor loads primarily on health satisfaction, with two economic satisfaction variables also showing moderate loadings. The second factor loads almost exclusively on satisfaction with economic situation--standard of living, and savings and investments. The third factor loads on satisfaction with the residential environment--neighborhood, community, and dwelling unit. The fourth factor loads on spare time activities, and things done with family and friends; satisfactions with the economic situation load _negatively_ on this factor.

Next we examined the interrelationships among the factors for the three age groups and their variances, using COFAMM to generate the test statistic for this hypothesis, and using the same model as was defined to test the previous hypothesis of equal factor loadings, except for added constraints to force equality of the variances of, and interrelationships between, factors. The goodness-of-fit statistic is X^2 = 150.9 with df = 127; the difference between this and the previous model is significant (X^2 = 44.4, df = 20, p = .001). We therefore conclude that the factor relationships are different at the different age levels.

The meaning of these differences becomes clear in Table 3-2, where the variances for each factor are shown, as well as the correlations between factors. The major difference is the estimated variance of factor 1, which was found to be related primarily to satisfaction with health: for those age 65 and older, the variance is more than three times the variance for those age 24-44. The variance on factor 2--primarily economic satisfaction--declines with age, and the correlation of factors 1 and 2 also declines for those age 65 and older.

Third analysis: Replication with 1978 data
_____

Our third analysis essentially replicates the second analysis, but used data from the 1978 Quality of Life study, which included the same domain satisfaction measures as the 1971 data. Since the general procedures have already been described, the findings will be summarized briefly.

The EFAP analysis showed that three factors gave a clearly inadequate fit for one age group (those age 45-64: X^2 = 47.22, df = 25, p = .005) and a marginal fit for the other two age groups (.05 < p < .10). Four factors yielded adequate fits (p > .10) in all three age groups, and also simplified the interpretation of subsequent analyses; thus, analyses based on four factors will be reported here.

In the COFAMM analysis, the model that constrains the factor loadings to be equal for each of the three age groups _is_ acceptable (p = .137). (It should be noted that in a first estimation of the model we did include the youngest age group--18 through 24 year olds--and found again an inadequate fit for the similarity of the factors.) A significantly worse fit is produced by the model that constrains not only the factor loadings but also the variances and interrelationships of the factors to be equal. Therefore we conclude that the variances and/or covariances of the latent factors are unequal across age levels.

Summary and Discussion

In this chapter we addressed a difference of opinion about the structure of subjective well-being, as defined by satisfactions with domains of life, and its stability across age levels. Andrews and Withey (1976) and Campbell et al. (1976) presented evidence based on national data which led them to conclude that the structure of well-being was largely independent of age. However, Cutler (1979) performed a reanalysis of the data collected by Campbell et al. and concluded that substantial age-related variations were reflected in the results. The age-stability of the concept is a critical issue, bearing on the suitability of this concept and its present measures for studies of the life span, and the disconcerting divergence of interpretations calls for a resolution.

We have carried the previous analyses somewhat further, changing some of the procedural and some of the conceptual features of the factor analytic procedure. After performing three different age-specific structural analyses based on data from two national studies of the American population we arrived at a mixed verdict: some similarities and some dissimilarities seems to characterize the structures at different age levels.

Let us summarize our various departures from those traditional procedures, that we believe are inadequate, and the impact of these departures on our findings and conclusions. Most critically, using the algorithm developed by Sorbom and Joreskog (1976), we performed confirmatory factor analyses, specifying several complex hypotheses representing various levels of factorial invariance and testing their fit to the observed data. This contrasts with exploratory factor analysis procedures to estimate parameters and then "eyeballing" them for similarities without exact statistical guidelines, the procedure followed by the previous investigators of this issue. In each case, the confirmatory factor analysis procedure takes the entire matrix of relationships into account when estimating the goodness-of-fit rather than relying on a few salient features, as Cutler's analysis did. For example, Cutler examined only factor loadings of .5 or more for identification of factors.

Another advantage of using the procedures designed by Sorbom and Joreskog is that they employ unstandardized measures of relationships and match the solution of each age group to maximize convergence with other age groups. As Cunningham (1978) points out, this is critical if one is to arrive at meaningful comparisons of factor analysis results at various age levels. In fact, one of the major differences we found at the level of factor interrelationships referred to factor variance and would presumably not have surfaced had we used the standardized measures of relationships.

Turning from these methodological issues to our findings, what conclusions can we draw about the similarity of the structure of well-being across age levels, and what implications do these findings have with respect to comparing levels of well-being across age groups? The findings from our three replications are quite consistent and can be summarized as follows.

First, there appears to be a common set of latent factors underlying reported levels of satisfaction with a variety of the domains, at least for people in the range of 25 to 74 years old. Younger people (age 18-24) appear to have a divergent set of latent factors, which may reflect the transitional nature of young adulthood before commitments are made to major roles such as careers and marriages. Such an age interpretation (rather than a cohort interpretation) is further supported by the occurrence of this difference in the data from both 1971 and 1978. A divergent set of latent factors may also be found among those age 75 and older. However, the size of the sample on which this apparent difference is based is small; so small, indeed, that we did not even try to confirm it in our second and third analyses, where instead we combined those age 75 and older with those age 65-74. The similarity of the factors for the restricted age range implies that basic dimensions of subjective well-being--economic satisfaction, health satisfaction, residential satisfaction, interpersonal/leisure satisfaction--measure the same concept for that age range and that they are therefore suitable for age investigations.

Second, we found that although a common set of underlying factors could adequately explain the structure of the observed variables in the age range of 25-74, the variances and interrelationships of those underlying factors themselves were significantly different even across this limited age range. In particular, a factor related primarily to health satisfaction was found to have increasing variance among older age groups, and to have a lower correlation with an economic satisfaction factor among those age 65 and older.

An implication of this latter finding is that, although the specific factors seem to be the same for respondents varying in age between 25 and 75 and thus may be used for the study of age differences in the level of subjective well-being, there are differences in the distributions of those satisfaction factors and in the degree to which satisfaction in one basic area of life is related to satisfactions in other basic areas. In other words, on a conceptual level, the interplay between specific satisfaction factors varies somewhat across age levels.

At the same time it bears noting that the use of an index of overall satisfaction formed by adding the various domain satisfaction measures would probably not introduce any major errors. It is known (Wilks, 1938) that the introduction of weights as they would be used for adjusting for age differences results in an index that differs little from an equally weighted additive index, under generally encountered conditions.

Table 3-1

Factor Loadings for Eleven
Satisfaction Items on Four Factors,
Constrained Equality across Three Age Groups

	Factor 1	Factor 2	Factor 3	Factor 4
Satisfaction with:				
Community	.044	-.021	.698	0.0[a]
Neighborhood	0.0[a]	-.024	.753[a]	-.041
Dwelling unit	.038	.165	.496	0.0[a]
Life in U.S.	.048	0.0[a]	.299	.156
Useful education	.219	.123	0.0[a]	.097
Spare time activities	.126	.097	-.155	.635[a]
Health	.765[a]	0.0[a]	-.231	0.0[a]
Standard of Living	.331	1.077[a]	-.007	-.467
Savings	.329	.538	-.028	-.152
Friends	0.0[a]	0.0[a]	0.0[a]	.547
Family	0.0[a]	.152	0.0[a]	.448

Note: The "loadings" are the regression coefficients for predicting
observed variables from the latent factors. The variances of
the satisfaction items for the entire sample, and the
weighted average of the variances of the factors across the
three age groups, were used to standardize these loadings.

[a] Constrained values. The highest loadings from EFAP analyses
were set to unstandardized values of 1.0, and the lowest
values to 0.0.

Table 3-2

Variances and Correlations of
Factors for Each of Three Age Groups

Age Group	Factor	Variances	Correlations		
			1	2	3
	1	.860			
24-44	2	3.428	.426		
	3	1.386	.612	.479	
	4	.905	.532	.667	.453
	1	1.411			
45-64	2	2.538	.508		
	3	1.365	.464	.503	
	4	.796	.563	.653	.549
	1	2.920			
65+	2	2.378	.144		
	3	1.229	.391	.391	
	4	.938	.549	.631	.488

CHAPTER 4

AGE AND SATISFACTION *

It is part of our popular wisdom that the later years are not the best part of life. When asked to choose the life stage which is the best, only a very small portion of an adult cross-section opts for the later years, while a considerable minority terms the later years actually the worst (Harris and associates, 1976). These views are largely shared by the aged respondents themselves.

On the other hand, when adults are asked to evaluate their own lives, a different pattern of findings emerges. The general tendency seems to be for older respondents to report higher satisfaction than do middle-aged or even young respondents. This finding has been reported in different research areas. In the area of occupational psychology a strong relationship between age and work satisfaction has been documented by Quinn et al. (1974) for eight national surveys and has been investigated by various authors (e.g., Gibson and Klein, 1970; Glenn et al., 1977; Hunt and Saul, 1975; Schwab and Heneman, 1977). In research on marriage and the family, marital satisfaction has been charted across the family life cycle and thereby indirectly across age. The relationship is often reported as curvilinear--a decline in satisfaction over the first years of the family life cycle followed by a gradual upswing in the later stages--although the evidence is not entirely consistent (Gilford and Bengtson, 1979; Rollins and Cannon, 1974; Rollins and Feldman, 1970; Schram, 1979; Spanier et al., 1975).

Campbell et al. (1976) found fairly linear age-related increases in satisfaction in almost all areas (such as housing, community, nonwork activities, and savings) and even with life in general; only with regard to health and happiness did they find an actual decrease. In fact, they were so impressed with this increase in satisfaction across a variety of life domains that they postulated it to be a general phenomenon. Other research, however, examined sex differences and noted that the increase in satisfaction was not as strong for women as for men (e.g., Spreitzer and Snyder, 1974; Schwab and Heneman, 1977).

The present chapter is designed to assess the generality of an age-related increase in satisfaction by means of replications across a diversity of life domains and across several nationwide cross-sectional surveys.

The relationship between age and satisfaction, if established, will of course go only one step towards an explanation, since chronological age reflects the effects of a multitude of variables that are correlated with it; any one or a combination of these could actually cause the association between age and satisfaction. One of the major distinctions to be made is that between aging and cohort effects: aging effects are associated with the length of time since birth, including biological, psychological and social

*A modified version of this chapter was previously published in Research on Aging, 1981, 3, 142-165.

35

changes. Cohort effects, on the other hand, are associated with being of a particular age at a particular time in history. No final resolution between these two classes of effects is possible with the cross-sectional data that are available for the present analyses. But even if cohort or aging effects could be identified, many explanations for either type of effect would still remain possible. Some of the specific explanations can be tested with the available data and the nature of these specific explanations, in turn, may shed some light on whether the age differences amount to a cohort or aging effect (Glenn et al., 1977).

Possible explanations of the relationship between age and satisfaction can be subsumed under two of the categories discussed by Campbell and his colleagues (1976): (1) subjective orientation and adjustment processes, and (2) objective improvement of the external situation. We begin by reviewing explanations related to subjective processes. Among these, Campbell et al. highlighted aspirations and expectations, which they found to decline with age. Whether such a decline is interpreted as resignation (Wright and Hamilton, 1978) or as realistic assessment (Herzberg et al., 1957), it is presumed to lessen the discrepancy between what is attained and what is hoped for and thereby increase the resulting satisfaction. Other aspects of a re-orientation related to age include an increased importance of religious values (Moberg, 1965). Such a change may well provide a clue to the relative satisfaction of many older people, since religiosity tends to be positively related to life satisfaction and mental health (Gurin et al., 1960; Hadaway, 1978; Spreitzer and Snyder, 1974).

Another adaptive mechanism of a purely psychological nature is suggested by Zajonc's (1968) work on the effect of mere exposure and is also implied by Campbell et al.'s discussion of the relationship between age and satisfaction. Zajonc has shown that the level of liking for an object is a function of familiarity which is related to the length of exposure. It could thus be argued that older people are more satisfied with various conditions of their life simply because they have spent more time under those particular conditions. For example, since on the average they have lived longer in their residence than younger people, they would presumably be more satisfied with their house and their community as well as with related aspects such as standard of living or neighbors. In a similar vein, students of job satisfaction (e.g. Herzberg et al., 1957; Hunt and Saul, 1975; Schwab and Heneman, 1977) have paid considerable attention to job tenure as an explanation of the relationship between job satisfaction and age. These studies tend to show that tenure explains some but by no means all of the relationship.

Finally, explanations which imply a more superficial adaptive mechanism refer to older people's increased tendency to conform (Klein, 1972; Klein and Birren, 1972). Specifically, it has been noted that older respondents are more inclined to respond to survey questions in a manner which they believe meets with the approval of others, or what Crowne and Marlowe (1964) have termed social desirability (Campbell et al., 1976). According to this hypothesis, older respondents would be more likely to express high satisfaction than young ones to the extent that they believe that such answers are the ones desired.

Similarly, it has been reported that older respondents exhibit more of an acquiescence response set than younger ones (Kogan, 1961; Murphy and Foley, 1979): they are more likely to agree with a survey statement regardless of its content. Although reporting satisfaction is not the same as agreeing with a given statement, it carries some of the same flavor of conforming to perceived expectations.

A second category of explanations for the age-related increase in satisfactions refers to improvements in the objective situation. In terms of particular life domains this means that unsatisfactory marriages have been dissolved (Campbell et al., 1976) or have improved once the burden of child rearing is relinquished (Deutscher, 1964), that jobs have become better with regard to salary level, security, pace, supervisory power, and use of skills (Campbell et al., 1976; Quinn et al., 1974; Wright and Hamilton, 1978), or that housing has improved as the starter home is replaced by increasingly prestigious homes, and so on.

A particularly interesting improvement refers to diminishing stress in later years that presumably results from fewer major life events such as marriage or divorce, change of job or residence, birth of a child, loss of spouse or friend, or unemployment. Although listings of major life events traditionally include a variety of specific experiences--some with a positive, some with a negative, and many with an ambiguous connotation; some voluntary, some involuntary--all of them may be viewed as stressful because of the change that they necessitate (Holmes and Rahe, 1967; Hultsch and Plemons, 1979). Indeed, the sheer number of them has been found to relate negatively to indicators of mental health by some (e.g., Myers et al., 1972), while others reported mental health to be related only to the number of negative events (Dekker and Webb, 1974; Pykel, 1974). The number of events declines quite markedly across the life span (Dekker and Webb, 1974; Duncan and Morgan, 1980; Uhlenhuth et al., 1974), suggesting that the bulk of major events happens in young adulthood and life stabilizes rapidly thereafter.[*] Older people themselves seem to experience life as less burdensome and less trying than younger people, since in the two Quality of Life surveys to be discussed below they rate life as less hard and less tied down on a set of semantic differential scales, as shown in negative correlations between age and those ratings that range from -.17 to -.22. It thus seems possible that at least part of the increased subjective well-being reported by older respondents could be accounted for by the lesser disruption of their daily lives from life events and related strains.

However, not all changes coming with old age represent objective improvements. Some changes clearly represent declines. The foremost example is health. Among people over 65 more than 40 percent report limitations in activities due to health or physical condition compared to somewhat over 10 percent in the total population (U.S. Department of HEW, 1979) and about 85 percent report at least one chronic disease (Shanas and Maddox, 1976). This

---

[*] Some critics have pointed out that the typical lists of life events are predominantly probing for events of young adulthood and therefore the decrease by age may be an artifact of the measurement device (Rabkin and Struening, 1976). Also, the decline appears particularly marked for positive and ambiguous events but much less clear for negative events (Duncan and Morgan, 1980).

worsening of health is in fact so strong that it produces the clear decline in
health satisfaction which appears to be the only clearly negative relationship
with age (Campbell et al., 1976). Given the pervasive impact of health on
various areas of life, health may well affect satisfaction with other domains
and certainly with life in general. Another fairly obvious example of a loss
in objective quality of life is the reduction in income after retirement.
Although income increases within the younger age groups, an aggregate decrease
sets in after the age of 55 (U.S. Bureau of the Census, 1976). Adjustment
for family size is likely to mitigate the effect somewhat, since older people
have smaller families to support; but the fact remains that people over 65 are
still overrepresented among the population in poverty (U.S. Bureau of the
Census, 1979). Also, older people tend to have less education. However, this
latter explanation represents more of a cohort than an age difference.

   The purpose of this chapter is two-fold. First, we will examine the
generalizability of the positive relationship between age and satisfaction
that was observed by Campbell et al. Second, insofar as relevant measures are
available we will test some of the specific hypotheses that have been
suggested to explain the relationship. For this second purpose, we used the
data collected by Campbell et al. in 1971 and the replication of that study by
Campbell and Converse in 1978 (Campbell and Converse, 1978). For the first
purpose we used in addition to these two data sets the set of social indicator
studies conducted by Andrews and Withey in 1972 in combined form; a combined
set of the seven General Social Surveys conducted annually from 1972 through
1978 by the National Opinion Research Center; a combined set of three Omnibus
surveys conducted by the Survey Research Center between 1973 and 1975; an
Omnibus study conducted in 1976 by the Survey Research Center; and a social
indicator study of the Detroit area.' Only respondents between 25 and 90
years old are included in these analyses, since the structural analysis
reported in the previous chapter suggest that the satisfaction variables may
have a different meaning for the youngest age groups.

Findings

Generality of the age-satisfaction relationship

   The strengths and significance levels of the relationships between age
and various satisfactions were examined by means of standardized regression
coefficients, which are displayed in Table 4-1. Since these coefficients
capture only the linear component of the relationship, eta values were also
calculated, with the age variable bracketing 10 year segments (data not
shown). Eta values indicate the strength of any form of relationship. By
comparing eta values and regression coefficients an assessment can be made as
to how much of the total relationship is lost by restricting it to a linear
form. On the average, little difference between these values are evident,
particularly if the eta values are corrected for shrinkage due to the ratio
between number of categories and number of respondents (Kerlinger and

---

   ' For more details on the studies and measures refer to the introductory
chapter and Appendix A.

Pedhazur, 1973); this finding suggests general linearity of the relationships. The largest differences occur for family and marriage satisfactions and for happiness and life satisfaction, but even there the size of the differences are inconsistent across data sets.

A cursory examination of Table 4-1 reveals that there is no entirely uniform relationship with age. Although most relationships--except the ones involving health satisfaction--are positive, they vary in strength and are not always statistically significant. Two factors appear to contribute to the variation in strength of the relationship. First, the average regression coefficient varies by data set; it is somewhat higher in the Quality of Life, the Detroit Social Indicator, and the 1976 Omnibus studies than in the Social Indicator, the General Social Surveys, and the 1973-1975 Omnibus studies. In our analysis of the readily available hypotheses (such as question or response scale format, presentation of the questions as a battery or spread out throughout the questionnaire) we found that none of them accounted for these observed differences between data sets.

A second source of difference is the particular domain of life with which satisfaction is expressed. As shown in Table 4-1, satisfaction with some of the domains is quite strongly related to age and the strength is also reasonably consistent across data sets. Examples are housing, community, and work; satisfaction in those areas increases considerably with age. Satisfaction with health is also strongly and consistently related to age; but in this case the relationship is negative, reflecting a clearcut decrease in satisfaction with increasing age. Other areas of life such as finances, standard of living, and leisure time, show in some instances strong relationships with age, but the relationships are less consistent across data sets. Finally, the measures of global well-being--satisfaction with life and happiness--as well as satisfaction with interpersonal domains--family, marriage, and friends--show coefficients which are inconsistent across data sets and quite often fairly low. Note also that the decline in happiness paired with an increase in life satisfaction as reported by Campbell et al. (1976) is not consistently replicated.

Although some have suggested that sex differences exist in the relationship between age and satisfaction, we found little evidence in support of this claim. We performed our analysis separately for both males and females (data not shown) and found little difference in the relationship between age and satisfaction from what we observed in our analysis of the total sample. The only difference that we observed was that magnitude of the coefficients was slightly lower for the females than for the males.

In conclusion, when examining these data sets a positive relationship between age and feelings of subjective well-being emerges for several domains of life. The relationship is therefore generalizable beyond satisfaction with any one particular area, although the phenomenon is hardly as omnipresent as judged by Campbell et al. (1976) exclusively on the basis of their own data. Interestingly, the replication of the Quality of Life study in 1978 shows equally strong age-relationships as their original study.

In the remaining part of this paper we will attempt to explain this age-related increase in subjective well-being. We will use only the two Quality of Life studies, since in these studies the relationship is present with reasonable strength, and measures are available that are relevant for testing the hypothesized explanations.

Explanations of the age-satisfaction relationship

In examining the contribution of the various hypothesized explanations we assume a causal model of the following form:

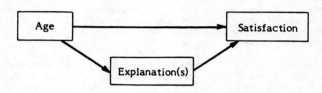

In other words, we postulate these explanations to be causally intervening between age and a particular domain satisfaction.[10] The explanatory power of such an intervening concept is tested in a multiple regression of the particular domain satisfaction, in which an indicator of the explanatory concept is included as a predictor along with age. The usefulness of the explanation is then assessed by the degree of reduction in the regression coefficient between age and the particular domain satisfaction when the intervening variable is included (Kerlinger and Pedhazur, 1973, p.314ff). Of course, indicators referring to each substantive explanation must be tested separately, if the effect of that particular explanation is to be assessed. On the other hand, if the total power of all explanations is to be determined, indicators for all of them need to be tested simultaneously, since the various explanations are likely to be related to each other.[11]

This analytic strategy led to a set of regressions for each domain

---

[10] We use "explanation" in its popular meaning, as opposed to "description." It deserves mentioning that in the scientific community the term "explanation" is often used for the situation in which a causally prior variable accounts for the association between two variables, while the term "interpretation" refers to the instance where a causally intervening variable accounts for the association of the two variables (Rosenberg, 1968). The explanations to be tested here are all of the interpretative form.

[11] Given the cross-sectional nature of the data these tests cannot conclusively establish the causal role of any particular concept but only document the consistency of the data with the hypothesis.

satisfaction. In each regression a particular domain satisfaction was regressed on age plus one or several indicators referring to potential explanations. Specifically, indicators were introduced (a) separately for each subjective explanation, (b) simultaneously for all subjective explanations, (c) separately for each situational explanation, (d) simultaneously for all situational explanations, (e) simultaneously for all the above explanations which produced any reduction in the age-satisfaction relationships. Tables 4-2 and 4-3 present the standardized regression coefficients between age and each domain satisfaction after introducing the controls in the order described above. Comparisons between the bivariate coefficients (given in the first column of the tables) and the multivariate coefficients, therefore, indicate whether the data are consistent with the explanations which are controlled in each specific analysis.

        Subjective orientation and adjustment processes. As described above, several subjective processes were hypothesized to explain the relationship between age and satisfactions. Specifically, it was argued that older respondents' higher religious inclinations, their adaptation over time, and their eagerness to please and agree may account for their relatively high reported satisfactions. A first look at the total explanatory power of the entire set of hypothesized explanations is therefore provided by a multiple regression analysis in which indicators for all explanations are included simultaneously (Table 4-2: Column 5; Table 4-3: Column 4). Only explanatory variables that did produce a modification of the relationship in preliminary analyses were included: this excluded a few measures of expectations and a rough measure of acquiescence in the form of the number of "agree"-responses to our attitudinal items. Standardized regression coefficients of satisfactions on age, when all subjective process variables are controlled, indicate that for many satisfaction variables a part of the original relationship is explained by this set of subjective processes. Except for the originally negative relationships most coefficients are reduced in strength, some even to a non-significant level.

        Separate regression analyses for each set of variables referring to a distinct explanation provide additional insight into the contribution of each single explanation (Table 4-2: Columns 2 through 4; Table 4-3: Columns 2 and 3). Increased religiosity among older adults provides a part of the explanation. Responses to three different questions on religious commitment are available in the 1971 survey; two of them were also asked in 1978. One question about the frequency of attendance at religious services and one on personal religious commitment ("In general, how religious-minded would you say you are?") are included in both surveys; in 1971 respondents were additionally asked how important religion is to them ("How important is having a strong religious faith?"). The responses to all these questions yield moderate relationships with age (product-moment correlation coefficients range from .14 to .18). When the set of these religious indicators is statistically controlled, a moderate reduction in the age-satisfaction relationships is observed, which occurs consistently across almost all domain satisfactions. We conclude that increasing religiosity is not a complete explanation of the relationship between age and satisfaction, but that it explains a consistent portion of the relationship.

        Another factor which contributes to the explanation of the relationship between age and satisfaction refers to the time spent in the present residence

and the adaptation process which presumably ensues. In both Quality of Life
surveys questions were included about how long the respondents had lived in
their present house and community; and the number of years reported show the
expected relationship with age. The bivariate relationships between age and
satisfactions are reduced somewhat when these variables are controlled. As
expected, reductions are more noticeable for coefficients involving
satisfaction with residence, economic status, and friendships, since we had
only measures of time spent in residency and in community available for our
analyses.

Perhaps the most critical psychological explanation is provided by the
desire of older persons to respond in socially acceptable ways. An index of
social desirability is formed from six items, which were selected from the
Social Desirability Scale developed by Crowne and Marlowe (1964) and included
in the 1971 Quality of Life Survey. Three of the items paraphrase socially
acceptable behaviors and measure social desirability by agreement, and three
paraphrase socially unacceptable behaviors and measure social desirability by
disagreement. (For a more complete discussion of the index see Campbell et
al., 1976.) Controlling on this index consistently reduces the coefficients
between age and each domain satisfaction. In other words, the age-related
increase in satisfactions is to a considerable degree explained by the greater
eagerness among the aged to give socially acceptable responses. The effect is
most pronounced for satisfactions with family, marriage, spare time, and life.
These are also the domains where such an effect is most likely since social
sanctions against not being satisfied with one's family and spouse and even
life are probably stronger than sanctions against not being satisfied with
one's house, community, finances or health.

Objective improvement of the external situation. An aspect of life which
appears to reflect an improvement as people get older, is the declining number
of major life events. The Quality of Life study conducted in 1978 contains an
extensive set of questions probing the frequency of 30 different life events
over the five years preceding the interview. The list is based on the scale
proposed by Holmes and Rahe (1967). Cognizant of suggestions that available
weighting procedures provide insignificant improvements (Chiriboga, 1978;
Lorimor, Justice, McBee, and Weinman, 1979), a simple sum of reported life
events was used here, which shows the predicted relationship with age (r =
-.40). But can this decline in the number of presumably disruptive events
account for the increased satisfaction with life and its various domains
experienced by older Americans? The results of a set of regression analyses
in which the number of life events was entered as an additional predictor
variable (Table 4-3: Column 5) suggest that the number of recent life events
does provide at least a partial explanation, since the effect of age on
satisfaction is weakened across all satisfaction variables except the few
which were originally negative (i.e., happiness and satisfaction with
health).[12]

Ratings of life on two semantic differential scales, "Free-Tied down" and

[12] Since the number of positive and ambiguous events are related much more
strongly to age than the number of negative events, we also conducted the
regression just for these events; overall this resulted in lesser reduction of
the age-satisfaction coefficients.

"Easy-Hard," corroborate the observed decline in numbers of life events and the presumably related stress: Older respondents are more likely to rate their lives as free and as easy than are younger ones. When the two variables are included in the regression analysis, rather substantial reductions in the relationships between age and satisfaction are observed (Table 4-2: Column 6; Table 4-3: Column 6). We conclude from this result that the lesser burdens and constraints experienced in later life do indeed contribute to the high satisfaction among the aged. While the two semantic differential measures contain an evaluative component which could make the observed age effect nothing more than another expression of the higher satisfaction among the elderly and the explanation provided by them tautological, this does not appear to be a realistic alternative hypothesis; eight additional semantic differentials which carry a similar evaluative connotation and are included in the same battery of questions do not show any age effects.

However, these objective improvements are to some degree offset by certain conditions that are actually worse for older people, such as health, income, or education. These observations tend to vitiate the claim that the increasing satisfaction displayed by older individuals generally reflects their improved living conditions. When the effects of health, family income, and education on the relationship between age and satisfactions are empirically tested, it is actually found that these specific instances of a relatively unfavorable objective situation suppress an even more substantial association between age and satisfactions.

Let us consider the evidence in somewhat greater detail. A measure of functional health was used in both Quality of Life surveys. The measure consists of two questions, resulting in a four-point functional health scale (1=Health problems that keep from doing lots of things; 2=Health problems that keep from doing certain things; 3=Health problems, but can do almost anything; 4=No particular health problem). Correlations between this health rating and age are $r = .38$ and $r = .35$ in the two surveys. Family income was measured by a question providing a showcard with 17 income categories; for analysis purpose, the midpoint dollar amount was assigned to each category. A slight decline in income with age is apparent in both Quality of Life surveys ($r = -.13$ and $r = -.10$). To be sure, these effects are not large, but they are noticeable and they are further registered by the older respondents themselves, who are more likely to report than younger ones that their "financial situation has been getting worse" ($r = .13$ in the General Social Surveys). Although the absolute dollar amount of family income would appear to be of less consequence than the income adjusted for need, it apparently is the former which is registered by the older respondents as worsening financial situation, since income level adjusted for family size does not decline with age. Finally, educational attainment was measured by the number of years of schooling that the respondent had completed. Of course, none of these measures is truly objective, since they are self-reports, and therefore open to bias; however, they deal with important factual information and thus would be expected to be recalled rather accurately. For example, self-reports of health are usually found to be quite closely related to assessments resulting from medical examinations (Balamuth, 1965; Maddox, 1962; Maddox and Douglas, 1973; Tissue, 1972).

When the three variables--health, family income, and education--are included in the regression equations predicting satisfaction measures (Table

4-2: Column 7; Table 4-3: Column 7), the standardized regression coefficients between age and satisfactions are actually strengthened compared to the respective bivariate coefficients. In concrete terms, if health, income, and education were not lower among older than among younger respondents, older respondents would be even higher compared to younger ones in their reported satisfactions. Technically, health, income, and education are said to "suppress" the relationship between age and satisfactions.

When the indicators of the objective situation discussed thus far are included simultaneously in a regression analysis (Table 4-2: Column 8; Table 4-3: Column 8), the relationships between age and satisfactions tend to be lower than the bivariate relationships. This outcome depends of course on the specific selection of variables, some of which strengthen, some of which weaken the relationship. A different subset might well have affected the overall balance differently. However, even this limited set of indicators shows that in contrast to the hypothesis which gave rise to the argument that increased satisfaction among the aged reflects their improved life situation, the objective quality of life in older age is in many important respects actually worse; the objective situation is therefore unlikely to provide a general explanation for the positive relationship observed between age and satisfactions. On the contrary, if their objective situation were not worse in some regards, older respondents would display an even greater increase in their satisfactions than they now do. On the other hand, some aspects of life--in this case we examined the exposure to major life events and evaluations of life as hard and restricted--do seem to improve when people age, and these factors actually contribute to their increased satisfactions.

Finally, the entire set of objective and subjective explanations discussed here, with the exception of income, education, and health, were included simultaneously in the regression equations. Comparisons of the resulting regression coefficients of satisfactions on age (Table 4-2: Column 9; Table 4-3: Column 9) with the corresponding bivariate coefficients reveal many substantial reductions, which are considerably more marked than the ones resulting from any single or group of explanations considered so far. In fact, many of the coefficients become non-significant; and some which originally were not very strong even take a negative direction, implying less satisfaction among the older parts of the population. Only the very strongest relationships retain significant positive coefficients, and even these are reduced by a substantial amount. This means, first, that the entire set of explanations examined here does indeed account for a large part of the relationship between age and satisfactions and, second, that the explanatory variables explored here illuminate different aspects of the explanation since the reductions are generally more marked when all the explanatory variables rather than only one of them are simultaneously included in the regression equation.

Summary and Discussion

The purpose of this chapter was to document the degree of generality of the supposed increase in satisfaction and happiness with age and to test possible explanations of this relationship. Measures of overall satisfaction with life and happiness as well as measures of satisfaction with specific areas of life were examined in seven different data sets. It was found that satisfaction with housing, community, and work show consistently strong age-related increases. Satisfactions with other areas as well as overall satisfaction and happiness show less consistent and less strong effects, although with the exception of health satisfaction the direction of the relationships is almost always positive. Upon this evidence, the relationship was interpreted as generalizable across several but not all domains of life investigated in these seven surveys.

Explanations were sought by examining the original relationships between age and satisfactions for reductions after statistically controlling on hypothetical explanatory variables. From these explorations it was learned that in comparison to young respondents older people's increased tendency to be religious and increased eagerness to respond in a socially approved fashion contributes to their higher sense of subjective well-being. Also contributing to the age relationships are the decline in number of major life events encountered by older people and the sheer amount of time they have spent in a particular situation with the adaptation effects that presumably took place during that time. The age differences on the first two factors (religiosity, social desirability response pattern) cannot be solely attributed to age effects since they may also reflect the operation of cohort effects. However, we can more confidently attribute the effects of the latter two factors (decline in number of major life events and time spent in a particular situation) solely to age effects.

In contrast to these variables which appear to provide a partial explanation for the age-related increase in satisfaction, several factors were identified which worsen with age and which operate as "suppressor" variables to conceal even more pronounced age-related increases. Such factors are declining health, lower educational level, and lower family income.

Explanations were sorted into objective situational and subjective factors, in order to test the validity of two basic contentions: (a) that higher satisfaction of older respondents is caused by their objectively better situation; and (b) that higher satisfaction among the older respondents results from a psychological adaptation process. Although few truly objective data were available, since most of the data at hand were collected by self-report, and although the number of measures was limited, it became quite clear that the objective quality of life does not uniformly improve across the life cycle. While some of the factors which do improve, such as the lessening of burdens and constraints, seem to account for some of the increased satisfaction, other conditions which are in fact worsening serve to suppress the tendency of the older respondents to report even higher satisfactions.

Admittedly, no single explanation is able to provide a sufficient explanation for the entire relationship between age and satisfactions; rather, they all form part of the explanation. The moderateness of these effects is however counterbalanced by their consistency across domains and data sets: a small effect such as that of income, education, and health always produces a slight increase in strength of the relationship, and conversely, the small effect of religiosity is consistent in producing a slight reduction in the relationship. Moreover, the size of the effects need to be judged in the light of the operationalization of particular explanations, which is frequently in the form of one-item measures with attendant reliability problems and is sometimes only an approximation to the concept in question. Since we used data that had already been collected, we had no control over the design of the instrument.

Nevertheless, although none of the tested variables provides a sufficient explanation of the relationship in and of itself, the entire set goes a good part of the way towards accounting for the relationship. This has been demonstrated by the multivariate regression analyses in which all explanatory variables are controlled simultaneously (Table 4-2: Column 9; Table 4-3: Column 9), which indicated that most regression coefficients are reduced by a substantial amount of the variance and many of them become actually statistically non-significant.

TABLE 4-1

Relationships Between Age and Subjective Well-Being Variables,
Across Seven Surveys

	Bivariate Standard. regression coefficient, regressing subj. well-being variables on age							
	Quality of Life 1971	Quality of Life 1978	General Social Surveys 1972-78	Detroit Social Indicator 1974	Social Indicator Study 1972	Omnibus 1973-75	Omnibus 1976 "Terr.-Delight"	Omnibus 1976 "Comp.Diss. Comp.Sat."
Satisfaction with finances/income	.05 (1793)	.13** (3103)	.17** (9141)	.09* (1071)	.00 (1936)	.06** (3219)	NA	NA
Satisfaction with job	.16** (1018)	.20** (1852)	.14** (7097)	.17** (609)	.08* (1184)	.03 (2152)	NA	NA
Satisfaction with family life	.10** (1742)	.13** (3105)	-.09** (7723)	.16** (1046)	-.03 (1852)	NA	NA	NA
Satisfaction with marriage	.13** (1266)	.13** (2011)	.04* (5514)	.07 (719)	-.01 (812)	-.05 (867)	.13* (477)	.13* (433)
Satisfaction with spare time	.14** (1814)	.14** (3125)	-.04** (7710)	.16** (1072)	.06* (1917)	NA	NA	NA
Satisfaction with house/apartment	.26** (1815)	.24** (3130)	NA	.26** (1077)	.11** (1941)	NA	.16** (707)	.22** (607)
Satisfaction with community	.17** (1819)	.15** (3141)	.20** (7749)	.15** (1073)	.09** (1939)	NA	NA	NA
Satisfaction with friendships	.16** (1814)	.09** (3118)	.03* (7745)	NA	.05* (1936)	NA	.14** (707)	.22** (607)
Satisfaction with standard of living	.21** (1822)	.19** (3113)	NA	.17** (1068)	.03 (1940)	.05 (3222)	NA	NA
Satisfaction with health	-.23** (1774)	-.18** (3135)	-.23** (7748)	-.17** (1069)	-.24** (1947)	-.05* (2529)	-.19*** (707)	-.12* (607)
Satisfaction with life	.06* (1804)	.10** (3117)	NA	.09* (1068)	-.05 (1935)	NA	.04 (707)	.12* (607)
Happiness	-.05 (1810)	-.01 (3124)	.01 (9151)	.00 (1070)	-.07* (1955)	NA	-.09* (707)	.00 (607)
Average coefficient (exc. health sat.)	.13	.14	.06	.13	.02	.01	.14	.14

NOTE: High scores indicate high satisfaction or happiness. Figures in parenthesis indicate numbers of respondents for each coefficient; statistical significance levels are based on two thirds of the actual sample size to adjust for a presumed average design effect of 1.5. *p < .05, **p < .01. Labels for subjective well-being variables are approximate descriptions; more details about stems and response scales are provided in the text.

TABLE 4-2

Quality of Life Survey, 1971: Relationships Between Age and Subjective Well-Being Variables, Controlling on Explanatory Variables

	Bivar. stand. regress. coeff.	Standardized regression coefficient controlling on:							All Variables except Inc. Ed. and Health
		Subjective Variables				Situational Variables			
		Relig.	Length in Resid.(LR)	Soc.Des.	Relig. LR Soc.Des.	Life Evals.	Inc. Ed. Health	Inc. Ed. Health Life Eval.	
Satisfaction from finances	.05	.03	.03	.03	.00	-.04	.19**	.09**	-.09*
Satisfaction with job	.16**	.14**	.14**	.14**	.11*	.10*	.23**	.16**	.05
Satisfaction with family life	.09**	.07*	.06	.06	.01	.02	.13**	.04	-.06
Satisfaction with marriage	.13**	.11**	.16**	.09**	.11**	.07	.15**	.09*	.06
Satisfaction with spare time	.14**	.13**	.12**	.10**	.08*	.06	.20**	.12**	.01
Satisfaction with house/apartment	.26**	.25**	.24**	.23**	.22**	.20**	.30**	.24**	.17**
Satisfaction with community	.17**	.16**	.15**	.15**	.13**	.12**	.21**	.15**	.09**
Satisfaction with friendships	.16**	.14**	.14**	.12**	.10**	.10**	.19**	.12**	.04
Satisfaction with standard of living	.21**	.20**	.19**	.18**	.16**	.12**	.34**	.24**	.08*
Satisfaction with health	-.23**	-.24**	-.24**	-.24**	-.25**	-.27**	.05*	.02	-.29**
Satisfaction with life	.06*	.04	.04	.02	.00	-.03	.17**	.06	-.09**
Happiness	-.05	-.07*	-.07*	-.09**	-.11**	-.15**	.05	-.05	-.20**

Note: See Table 4-1.

TABLE 4-3

Quality of Life Survey, 1978: Relationships Between Age and Subjective Well-Being Variables, Controlling on Explanatory Variables

| | | Standardized regression coefficient controlling on: | | | | | | | |
| | | Subjective Variables | | | Situational Variables | | | | |
	Bivar. stand. regress. coeff.	Relig.	Length in Resid.	Relig. Length	Life Events	Life Eval.	Inc., Ed., and Health	Ed., Inc., Health, Life Events, Life Eval.	All Variables, except Inc., Ed., and Health
Satisfaction with income	.13**	.12**	.10**	.10**	.08**	.04	.22**	.08**	-.02
Satisfaction with job	.20**	.19**	.20**	.20**	.17**	.14**	.22**	.15**	.13**
Satisfaction with family life	.13**	.11**	.13**	.13**	.08**	.06**	.14**	.02	.03
Satisfaction with marriage	.13**	.11**	.12**	.10**	.10**	.07*	.15**	.06	.02
Satisfaction with spare time	.14**	.13**	.14**	.14**	.12**	.06**	.19**	.09**	.04
Satisfaction with house/apartment	.24**	.23**	.24**	.23**	.20**	.18**	.28**	.17**	.14**
Satisfaction with community	.15**	.14**	.13**	.13**	.12**	.10**	.16**	.07**	.06*
Satisfaction with friendships	.09**	.08**	.07*	.06**	.08**	.04	.11**	.03	-.01
Satisfaction with standard of living	.19**	.18**	.18**	.17**	.15**	.10**	.28**	.15**	.05
Satisfaction with health	-.18**	-.19**	-.18**	-.18**	-.22**	-.24**	.04	-.02	-.26**
Satisfaction with life	.10**	.08**	.10**	.10**	.07**	.00	.17**	.03	-.03
Happiness	-.01	-.03	-.01	-.02	-.04	-.10**	.06*	-.05*	-.12**

Note: See Table 4-1.

CHAPTER 5

EFFECTS OF ROLES AND RESOURCES
ON SUBJECTIVE WELL-BEING

In this chapter we examine the effect of roles and resources on subjective well-being. As mentioned in the introduction, previous research has shown resources such as income, health, education, and marital status to yield consistent although not very strong effects on subjective well-being among the aged as well as among the total population. At the same time, factors that we labeled sociodemographic in the introduction--sex and race-- show less consistent effects. There is further some scattered evidence suggesting that the impact of some of these factors may change as a function of age, although the few findings are again inconsistent.

This chapter provides replications of previous analyses, examining the impact of a set of standard resource and sociodemographic factors on subjective well-being. However, it extends those analyses by including systematic comparisons of the impact of these factors at different stages of the life span. Thus, the focus is on interactions of predictors and age on subjective well-being in addition to the main effects of the predictors. The result is a set of regression coefficients that indicate the difference or stability, respectively, of the impact of the resource factors across the life span.

In the previous chapter we used some of these resource factors (i.e., income, education, and health) and their differences by age as explanations for the relationship between age and satisfaction. In doing so, we assumed similar relationships between resources and subjective well-being across age levels. In the analyses to be reported below the focus is on the potentially different impact of these resources and roles at different age levels. In other words, the assumption of the previous chapter becomes the very topic of investigation in this chapter.

Method

Data

The following data sets were used in this chapter: the set of social indicator studies conducted in 1972 by Andrews and Withey; a combined data set consisting of the seven General Social Surveys conducted annually from 1972 through 1978 by the National Opinion Research Center (Davis et al., 1978); the social indicator study of the Detroit area (Rodgers et al., 1975); the Quality of Life survey conducted by Campbell et al. in 1971 (Campbell et al., 1975) and its replication in 1978 (Campbell and Converse, 1978). Only respondents

25 years old and older are included in these analyses, since our previous
analyses (Chapter 3) had suggested that very young respondents may conceive of
subjective well-being in a qualitatively different way.

Measures

Each of the studies contains one or two measures of global feelings of
well-being, i.e. satisfaction with life and happiness. The life satisfaction
measure is always a 7-point Likert-type scale; exact phrasing of question and
scale values are slightly different for some of the data sets; the happiness
measure is identical for all data sets, providing three scale positions "Very
happy," "Pretty happy," and "Not too happy." These two types of measures are
used as dependent variables in the analyses to follow. The predictors are a
set of variables representing roles and resources. Specifically, sex, race,
income, education, employment status, marital status, and health were
included. The scoring of the predictors is reported in the tables.

Analysis procedure

The impact of these predictors on overall subjective well-being was
evaluated by multiple regression analysis. While the major focus of these
analyses is on the older respondents, the more general question is clearly
concerned with the stability or change across age levels. Therefore, the
multiple regression analyses for the total samples were specified to include
as predictors not only the resource factors but additional dummy variables for
age levels and a set of interaction terms representing the interactive effect
of each resource factor and age level on overall well-being. Age levels were
specified as young (25-44), middle-aged (45-64) and older (65-97); two dummy
variables were specified to represent these age groups. Interaction terms
were formed as the product of the age dummy variables and the resource
variables, resulting in two terms per resource factor, corresponding to the
two age dummy variables. All resource variables and the 2 age dummy variables
were forced into a step-wise regression as predictors of subjective well-
being. However, the interaction terms were included only if the addition
resulted in an increase in explained variance of an F-value of 1.0 or higher.
If neither of the two interaction terms per predictor variable entered the
regression, the coefficients are identical across age levels. If, however, an
interaction term entered the equation, because it adds to the explained
variance, then the regression coefficients for the age levels are different by
the magnitude of the coefficient for the interaction term. The unstandardized
regression coefficients (Tables 5-1 through 5-6) may be understood as effects
of each predictor on overall subjective well-being when the effects of all
other predictors are controlled, measured as the amount of change in the
overall well-being scale that is associated with a one-unit change in the
predictor variable. For comparing effects of predictors across age levels or
across data sets these unstandardized coefficients have to be used. However,
if predictors within a given age group and data set need to be compared with
each other, standardized regression coefficients must be used. Standardized
coefficients are therefore included in the tables right below the
unstandardized coefficients.

Although these interpretations are fairly straightforward, the marking of the statistical significance is somewhat less conventional and requires some explanation. For the oldest age group asterisks indicate the level of statistical significance of the coefficients in the conventional way; for the middle-aged and the young age groups letter subscripts indicate whether the interaction term added a significant amount of explained variance. Coefficients with the same subscript in a row are not different at the .05 level of statistical significance from the coefficients for the older (65-97) age group.[13] Note also that this form of analysis does not result in separate significance estimates for the young and the middle-aged respondents; coefficients for these age groups are only evaluated as to whether they are significantly different from the coefficients for the oldest respondents.

                                 Findings

The results of the analyses are displayed in Tables 5-1 through 5-6. These tables reveal a remarkable level of consistency across the six data sets. The consistency is particularly noteworthy given the slight differences in measurement methods used to assess the variables involved, and this considerably raises our confidence in the findings.

Marital status has by far the strongest net effect on overall subjective well-being among the aged: the older respondents who are married feel better about their lives than the ones who are not presently married. This is shown by the effect of the dummy variable on overall well-being; the difference between being married and not presently married corresponds to roughly half a scale value on scales ranging from 1 through 5 for happiness and 1 through 7 for life satisfaction. Note also that the widowed respondents are not as different from single and divorced respondents as those who are currently married; this suggests that the higher well-being of the married reflects something about the actual marriage relationship rather than differences in the composition of the people who are getting and remain married from those who are not married. Among the middle-aged and young respondents being married has a very similar beneficial effect. In other words, the interaction effect is rarely significant, resulting thereby mostly in identical estimates of the regression coefficients.

Only self-reported health status achieves similar relative importance as marital status. However, this assertion has to remain more tentative, since only three of the seven data sets that are used here contained a health measure. An increase of roughly a quarter of a scale category in subjective well-being is associated with each scale point of the four-point health scales which are being used in the present analyses. Although we have to remain

---

[13] However, in some cases they are slightly different numerically because the variable entered the regression equation by having an F-value of at least 1.0 for explanatory power added during one of the regression steps and not falling below that value in subsequent steps, but did not reach the .05 level of statistical significance at the last step of the stepwise regression procedure.

equally tentative about age differences in the effect of health due to the few replications, contrary to many hypotheses there is no evidence in these data that health has a stronger impact on the subjective well-being of older respondents than on subjective well-being of other age groups.

Although income and education show a tendency to be positively correlated with subjective well-being, the net coefficients are so inconsistent and weak as not to warrant too much attention. This pattern of inconsistent and weak effects also holds for income and education in the other age groups. Of course, the independent effect of the two variables in a multivariate analysis is most likely curtailed due to the level of intercorrelation between the two variables (Gordon, 1968). Correlations between income and education ranged between .40 and .52 across our various data sets.

Sex and employment status show no effects on subjective well-being as reported by the older respondents. In other words, older women and men feel equally good about their lives, when differences in marital status, economic situation and health are statistically held constant. Likewise, employed and non-employed older respondents do not differ in their reported subjective well-being, when these other variables are controlled. Moreover, the effects of employment status and sex are no more substantial for the middle-aged and young respondents.

In contrast to these findings, a very interesting and consistent age pattern emerges for the effect of race on satisfaction: Race, which shows weak and inconsistent effects on overall well-being among the aged and the middle-aged respondents, appears to have a stronger impact among the young respondents. In several analyses young blacks report less happiness than young whites, while at the same time middle-aged and particularly older blacks do not differ systematically from older whites in their reports of happiness. For life satisfaction the evidence for this interaction is less clear; in only one of the data sets that contain a life satisfaction variable is this form of an interaction significant (in one additional data set it is in the predicted direction, but does not reach statistical significance.) Nevertheless, the evidence is suggestive that young blacks are less satisfied than young whites while older blacks are much less discrepant from older whites. Note also that this effect is net of any differences in income, education, or health as they might exist between the two races.

In sum, the interaction of race and age on happiness is the only interaction that consistently emerges from these analyses. The remaining predictors show similar effects across age levels, either in their strength or their weakness.

Summary and Discussion

This chapter replicated standard analyses in social-gerontology aimed at predicting morale from a number of roles and resources, and submitted those predictors to a systematic analysis of interactions with age. Only one replicable interaction was found. Race differences existed among young respondents. Young blacks report less happiness than young whites; little evidence for such a race difference exists among middle-aged and older respondents. While marital status and health are strong and replicable predictors of subjective well-being, their effects vary little by age group. Likewise, the lack of effects of sex and employment status varies little by age level. These findings suggest that the formation and change of subjective well-being through resources and roles is not very different at different age levels. We conclude therefore that a model of the formation and change of subjective well-being can be developed for the entire age range. Note however that the entire set of resource and role factors rarely accounts for more than 10 percent of the variance, and we are not ruling out the possibility that interactions exist among many other variables that we have not examined in our analysis.

Table 5-1

Detroit Social Indicator Study, 1973-74:
Effects of Socio-Demographic Characteristics
on Life Satisfaction and Happiness, by Age Group

Criteria:	Life Satisfaction (1=comp.dissat.;7=comp.sat.)			Happiness (1=not too happy; 5=very happy)		
Age	25-44	45-64	65-97	25-44	45-64	65-97
Predictors:						
Sex (1=male, 2=female)	.039[a]	.039[a]	.039[a] / .013	.136[a]	.136[a]	.136[a] / .052
Race (1=white, 5=black)	-.106[b]	.063[a]	.063[a] / .076	.036[a]	.036[a]	.036[a] / .049
Family Income (1=$2,000—17=$35,000+)	.011[a]	.011[a]	.011[a] / .031	.026[a]	.026[a]	.026[a]* / .083
Education (No. years completed)	.029[a]	.029[a]	.029[a] / .061	.010[a]	.010[a]	.010[a] / .025
Employment Status (1=working, 2=not working)	-.015[a]	-.015[a]	-.015[a] / -.005	.017[a]	.017[a]	.017[a] / .006
Marital Status I (1=married, 0=not married)	.540[a]	.540[a]	.540[a]* / .176	.515[a]	.515[a]	.515[a]* / .189
Marital Status II (1=widowed, 0=not widowed)	.059[a]	.059[a]	.059[a] / .013	.138[a]	.138[a]	.138[a] / .035
R^2, adj.		.051			.051	

Note: For each predictor, entries in the first line are unstandardized regression coefficients, entries in the second line (for the oldest group) are standardized regression coefficients. Identical superscript of coefficients across age levels mean that the respective interaction term is not significant at the .05 level. Thus, the presence of a 'b' or 'c' superscript indicates that the interaction term for that age group was significantly different from that of the 65-97 age group at the .05 level.

* p<.05

Table 5-2

General Social Surveys, 1972-1978: Effects
of Socio-Demographic Characteristics
on Happiness, by Age Group

| Criteria: | Happiness (1=Not too happy;5=Very happy) | | |
| | Age | | |
Predictors:	25-44	45-64	65-97
Sex (1=male, 2=female)	$.292^b$	$.108^a$	$.108^{a}$*
			.042
Race (1=white, 2=black)	$-.416^b$	$-.160^a$	$-.160^{a}$*
			-.039
Family Income, (in $1,000s, corrected for inflation)	$.008^a$	$.008^a$	$.008^{a}$*
			.057
Education (no. years completed)	$.012^b$	$-.008^a$	$-.008^a$
			-.020
Employment Status (0=working, 1=not working)	$-.062^b$	$.106^a$	$.106^a$
			.040
Marital Status I (1=married, 0=not married)	$.544^a$	$.544^a$	$.544^{a}$*
			.188
Marital Status II (1=widowed, 0=not widowed)	$-.058^a$	$-.058^a$	$-.058^a$
			-.014
Health (1=poor--4=excellent)	$.396^a$	$.328^b$	$.396^{a}$*
			.275
R^2, adj.		.130	

Note: For each predictor, entries in the first line are unstandardized
regression coefficients, entries in the second line (for the oldest
group) are standardized regression coefficients. Identical
superscript of coefficients across age levels mean that the
respective interaction term is not significant at the .05 level.
Thus, the presence of a 'b' or 'c' superscript indicates that the
interaction term for that age group was significantly different from
that of the 65-97 age group at the .05 level.

* p<.05

Table 5-3

Quality of Life Survey, 1978:
Effects of Socio-Demographic Characteristics
on Life Satisfaction and Happiness, by Age Group

Criteria:	Life Satisfaction (1=comp.dissat.;7=comp.sat.)			Happiness (1=not too happy; 5=very happy)		
Age	25-44	45-64	65-97	25-44	45-64	65-97
Predictors:						
Sex (1=male, 2=female)	$-.014^a$	$-.014^a$	$-.014^a$ / $-.015$	$.020^a$	$.020^a$	$.020^a$ / .009
Race (1=white, 2=black)	$-.067^a$	$-.067^a$	$-.067^a$ / $-.016$	$-.292^b$	$.020^a$	$.020^a$ / .005
Family Income (1=none--26=80,000+)	$.016^a$	$.016^a$	$.016^a$* / .068	$.013^a$	$.013^a$	$.013^a$* / .063
Education (0=none--17=17 yrs.or more)	$.009^a$	$-.038^b$	$.009^a$ / .023	$.011^a$	$.011^a$	$.011^a$ / .032
Employment Status (1=working, 2=not working)	$.030^a$	$.030^a$	$.030^a$ / .012	$-.045^a$	$-.045^a$	$-.045^a$ / $-.019$
Marital Status (1=married, 0=not married)	$.487^a$	$.487^a$	$.487^a$* / .182	$.443^a$	$.443^a$	$.443^a$* / .182
Marital Status (1=widowed, 0=not widowed)	$.299^a$	$.299^a$	$.299^a$* / .081	$.024^a$	$.024^a$	$.024^a$ / .007
Health (1=many problems, 4=none)	$.195^a$	$.195^a$	$.195^a$* / .166	$.131^a$	$.131^a$	$.131^a$* / .122
R^2, adj.		.074			.070	

Note: For each predictor, entries in the first line are unstandardized regression coefficients, entries in the second line (for the oldest group) are standardized regression coefficients. Identical superscript of coefficients across age levels mean that the respective interaction term is not significant at the .05 level. Thus, the presence of a 'b' or 'c' superscript indicates that the interaction term for that age group was significantly different from that of the 65-97 age group at the .05 level.

* p<.05

Table 5-4

Quality of Life Survey, 1971:
Effects of Socio-Demographic Characteristics
on Life Satisfaction and Happiness, by Age Group

Criteria:	Life Satisfaction (1=comp.dissat.;7=comp.sat.)			Happiness (1=not too happy; 5=very happy)		
Age	25-44	45-64	65-97	25-44	45-64	65-97
Predictors:						
Sex (1=male, 2=female)	.181[b]	-.121[a]	-.121[a]*	.098[a]	.098[a]	.098[a]*
			-.047			.040
Race (1=white, 2=black)	.015[a]	.015[a]	.015[a]	-.399[b]	.038[a]	.038[a]
			.003			.010
Family Income (0=none, 17=35,000+)	.041[b]	-.002[a]	-.002[a]*	.021[a]	.021[a]	.021[a]*
			-.008			.081
Education (0=nine--17/or/more years)	.009[a]	.009[a]	.009[a]	.016[a]	.016[a]	.016[a]
			.025			.044
Employment Status (1=working, 2=not working)	.019[a]	.019[a]	.019[a]	.031[a]	.031[a]	.031[a]
			.008			.013
Marital Status (1=married, 0=not married)	.701[a]	.701[a]	.701[a]*	.444[a]	.444[a]	.444[a]*
			.253			.171
Marital Status (1=widowed, 0=not widowed)	.324[a]	.324[a]	.324[a]*	.008[a]	.008[a]	.008[a]
			.089			.002
Health (1=many problems, 4=none)	.226[a]	.226[a]	.226[a]*	.160[a]	.160[a]	.160[a]*
			.193			.146
R^2, adj.		.103			.091	

Note: For each predictor, entries in the first line are unstandardized regression coefficients, entries in the second line (for the oldest group) are standardized regression coefficients. Identical superscript of coefficients across age levels mean that the respective interaction term is not significant at the .05 level. Thus, the presence of a 'b' or 'c' superscript indicates that the interaction term for that age group was significantly different from that of the 65-97 age group at the .05 level.

* p<.05

Table 5-5

Social Indicator Surveys, 1972:
Effects of Socio-Demographic Characteristics
on Life Satisfaction and Happiness, by Age Group

Criteria:	Life Satisfaction (1=terrible; 7=delighted)			Happiness (1=not too happy; 5=very happy)		
Age	25-44	45-64	65-97	25-44	45-64	65-97
Predictors:						
Sex (1=male, 2=female)	-.065^a	-.065^a	-.065^a / -.032	.079^a	.079^a	.079^a / .034
Race (1=white, 2=black)	-.067^a	-.067^a	-.067^a / -.019	-.341^a	-.341^a	-.341^a* / -.085
Family Income (1=<3,000—8=25,000++)	.083^b	.017^a	.017^a / .034	.061^a	-.002^b	.061^a* / .109
Education (no. years completed)	.028^a	-.011^a	.028^a* / .089	.035^a	.035^a	.035^a* / .100
Employment Status (1=working, 2=not working)	-.086^a	-.086^a	-.086^a / -.043	-.026^a	-.026^a	-.026^a / -.011
Marital Status I (1=married, 0=not married)	.511^c	.489^b	.054^a / .025	.404^a	.404^a	.404^a* / .162
Marital Status II (1=widowed; 0=not widowed)	.093^a	.093^a	.093^a / .032	.125^a	.125^a	.125^a / .038
R^2, adj.		.062			.059	

Note: For each predictor, entries in the first line are unstandardized regression coefficients, entries in the second line (for the oldest group) are standardized regression coefficients. Identical superscript of coefficients across age levels mean that the respective interaction term is not significant at the .05 level. Thus, the presence of a 'b' or 'c' superscript indicates that the interaction term for that age group was significantly different from that of the 65-97 age group at the .05 level.

* $p<.05$

Table 5-6

Ommibus Surveys, 1973-1975:
Effects of Socio-demographic Characteristics on
Life Satisfaction, by Age Group

| Criteria: | Life Satisfaction | | |
| | Life Satisfaction (1=terrible; 7=delighted) | | |
Age	25-44	45-64	65-97
Predictors:			
Sex (1=male, 2=female)	-.170[b]	.146[a]	.146[a]
			.061
Race (1=white, 2=black)	.073[a]	.073[a]	.073[a]
			.018
Family Income (1=<2,000, 18=>35,000)	.055[a]	.022[b]	.055[a]*
			.213
Education (no. years completed)	.029[a]	.029[a]	.029[a]*
			.082
Employment Status (1=working, 2=not working)	-.066[a]	-.066[a]	-.066[a]
			-.028
Marital Status (1=married, 0=not married)	.502[a]	.502[a]	.502[a]*
			.193
Marital Status (1=widowed, 0=not widowed)	.111[a]	.111[a]	.111[a]
			.031
R^2, adj.		.091	

Note: For each predictor, entries in the first line are unstandardized regression coefficients, entries in the second line (for the oldest group) are standardized regression coefficients. Identical superscript of coefficients across age levels mean that the respective interaction term is not significant at the .05 level. Thus, the presence of a 'b' or 'c' superscript indicates that the interaction term for that age group was significantly different from that of the 65-97 age group at the .05 level.

* p<.05

CHAPTER 6

EFFECTS OF SATISFACTION WITH ROLES AND RESOURCES
ON SUBJECTIVE WELL-BEING

This chapter explores predictions of overall subjective well-being from subjective evaluations of roles and resources. While the nature of the predictors is similar as in Chapter 5--major roles and resources traditionally examined in research on subjective well-being--the predictors are cast in subjective rather than objective terms. Not so much the purely quantitative variations of resources, which may mean very different things to different people, but the respondent's own assessment of his or her resources are at the core of this set of analyses. To take an obvious example, the absolute level of income may be of little consequence for overall subjective well-being, since higher incomes have the potential for creating increased needs and therefore leaving the individual struggling to make ends meet. On the other hand, the level of satisfaction with income, which indicates the sufficiency of whatever funds are available to cover the individual's needs, is most likely more critical in determining subjective well-being. Similar arguments may be made for the level of social contacts and relationships. As we have maintained in the introduction, not enough attention has been paid to researching the qualitative and subjective aspects of roles and resources and their impact on subjective well-being.

Concretely, variables measuring satisfaction with income, marriage, health, leisure, and the like are used in these analyses in order to predict overall subjective well-being, as measured by life satisfaction and happiness.

Here again, our focus is on determining whether the impact of each variable is different among people of different age groupings (25-44, 45-64, and 65-97). Thus, we will examine whether statistically significant interactions occur between various domain satisfactions and age in their effect on subjective well-being.

Data

The two Quality of Life Surveys, the Social Indicator Surveys, the Detroit Study, and the General Social Surveys were used for these analyses. Only respondent 25 years old or older are included in these analyses.

Measures

Each of the studies contains one or two measures of global feelings of well-being, i.e. satisfaction with life and happiness. The life satisfaction

measure is a 7-point Likert-type scale. However, exact phrasings of question
and scale values are slightly different for some of the data sets. The
happiness measure is identical for all data sets, providing three scale
positions "very happy," "pretty happy," and "not too happy." These two types
of measures are used as dependent variables in our analyses.

The predictors are represented by a set of measures which assess
satisfaction with particular domains of life. The domains are similar across
studies, but again, not all of them are phrased in exactly the same way, nor
do they use the same response scale. For example, some questions probe
"family life," while others ask about "things you do with your family"; or
some refer to "spare" time, others to "leisure" time.[14] Drawing on the
findings from our previous analyses of the open-ended questions and the
structural analyses we examined satisfactions with the following domains: (1)
economic situation (in some data sets this variable was a combination of
satisfaction with income and satisfaction with standard of living); (2)
residence (in some data sets this variable was a combination of satisfaction
of dwelling unit and of community); (3) interpersonal and leisure
satisfaction (a combination of satisfaction with family, friends, and leisure/
hobbies/spare time); (4) work; and (5) health. Satisfaction with political
and national issues was not included despite the frequency with which it was
mentioned as a source of unhappiness since such a question was asked in only
two of the surveys and did not show any strong relationship with overall well-
being in preliminary analyses. This procedure for selecting and specifying
predictors guarantees inclusion of the major domains that surfaced in Chapters
2 and 3 and reduces the multicollinearity problem through combining highly
interrelated domain satisfaction variables into indices.

Analysis procedures

The impact of standardized domain satisfaction ratings on overall
subjective well-being, operationalized by a rating of life satisfaction and a
rating of happiness, is evaluated by multiple regression analysis. While the
major focus of these analyses is on the older respondents, the more general
question is again concerned with the stability or change across age
levels. Analogous to the analytical procedure used in the previous chapter,
multiple regression analyses for the total samples were specified to include
as predictors not only the domain satisfactions but additionally dummy
variables for age levels and a set of interaction terms representing the
interactive effect of each domain satisfaction and age level on overall well-
being. While domain satisfaction and age dummy variables were forced into the
regression equation as predictors, the interaction terms were only included if
their addition resulted in an increase in the accounted variance of an F-value
of 1.0 or more. In the tables (Tables 6-1 through 6-5), regression
coefficients for the age levels are different by the magnitude of the
coefficient for the interaction term.

[14] Refer to Appendix A for details on question wording.

Findings

Before engaging in discussions of the substantive results, a general characteristic of these data needs to be pointed out: the impacts of domain satisfactions are generally stronger on life satisfaction than on happiness, and likewise a higher percentage of the variance in life satisfaction is explained by the domain satisfaction variables. This difference must be largely attributed to a method rather than a substantive effect, since the phrasing of the life satisfaction measures and their response scale is, of course, much more similar to the domain satisfaction measures than is the happiness measure. Given this likely interpretation, we will discuss the effects separately for each dependent measure.

Focusing first on the older respondents exclusively, satisfaction with economic conditions, which in several data sets includes income as well as standard of living, is the most powerful and consistent predictor across all data sets and for both the satisfaction and happiness measures. The standardized regression coefficients for economic satisfaction are almost invariably high and all but one are statistically significant. Thus, feeling at ease about one's financial and material situation is apparently critical for feeling happy and satisfied with one's life. This fact is not only reflected in the statistical correlations presented here, but is also recognized by the older respondents themselves, as shown in the responses to the open-ended questions reported in Chapter 2. There, we saw that economic concerns were among the most frequently mentioned reasons for happiness, unhappiness, and worries.

The impact of economic satisfaction varies little by age. That is, in most data sets a similar coefficient adequately describes the effect of economic satisfaction for all age groups; and in the few data sets where this is not true, the variation by age is inconsistent. The lack of age variation indicates that the subjective quality of economic conditions is about equally important for older, middle-aged, and young Americans' overall subjective well-being. This finding is quite consistent with the results to the open-ended questions discussed above: i.e., not only is economic satisfaction important at any age level, but for respondents of all ages this particular source is among the most frequently mentioned reasons for happiness, unhappiness, and worries.

The effect of marital satisfaction on subjective quality of life displayed in these analyses is somewhat less consistent although often of similar strength as the effect of economic satisfaction. In other words, satisfaction with marriage seems to have a less consistent impact on overall subjective well-being, particularly on happiness, than economic satisfaction. This again parallels the findings from the open-ended questions, where only a few older respondents named marriage as a source of happiness.

The age pattern of the impact of marital satisfaction, on the other hand, is fairly consistent across data sets. In about half of the analyses coefficients for the youngest age group are significantly different from those for the oldest age group; and in all these instances they are stronger for the youngest age group. The coefficients for the middle-aged are generally not significantly different from those of the oldest age group. These findings suggest that the degree of satisfaction young people get from their marital relationship has an impact on their subjective well-being which is substantial and stronger than its effect among older or middle-aged respondents.

Other domain satisfactions which contribute to the overall subjective well-being among older respondents are satisfaction with family, leisure, and friends. These satisfaction variables were combined into an index by averaging them, based on the investigations of the structure of subjective well-being (reported in Chapter 3) that suggested only one factor for interpersonal and leisure satisfactions.[15] In most data sets the index shows fairly strong, and in all but one instances statistically significant, coefficients.

The age pattern of the impact of leisure/interpersonal satisfaction on global well-being conforms with our expectations and with what we have learned from the analysis of the open-ended questions. The coefficients for the youngest age group tend to be lower than the ones for the oldest or middle-aged group, while these two latter age groups do not show a consistent pattern. It appears therefore that these combined sources of well-being are more important for older and middle-aged than for young age groups.

The understanding of the effect of leisure/interpersonal satisfaction at different age levels may be further improved if it is contrasted with the age pattern of the effect of work satisfaction. Unlike leisure/interpersonal satisfaction, work satisfaction shows a somewhat weaker impact on overall subjective well-being among older respondents than among younger ones. The relative importance of leisure/interpersonal satisfaction and work satisfaction can be assessed directly for the older respondents using the standardized regression coefficients. In several studies analyzed here leisure/interpersonal satisfaction shows a stronger effect on subjective well-being than work satisfaction. Thus, in spite of the fact that estimates of coefficients involving job satisfaction are based only on the respondents who are still holding a job, many of whom presumably do so because they prefer to remain working, job satisfaction is less consequential than leisure/interpersonal satisfaction at this stage of the life cycle. Moreover, if the age patterns of these two areas of satisfaction are compared based on the unstandardized regression coefficients, the effect of leisure/interpersonal satisfaction tends to be somewhat stronger among the older than among the younger respondents, while the effect of work satisfaction tends to be somewhat weaker among the older than the younger respondents.

Some domains of life which older respondents mentioned as of prime importance for their subjective well-being in response to the open-ended questions (Chapter 2) seem to have less of an effect on subjective well-being than expected. For example, satisfaction with health shows effects which are generally weaker although mostly statistically significant than effects of other domain satisfactions. Moreover, the effects of health satisfaction are often identical for all three age groups and certainly not stronger for the old. While ailing health as a threat to subjective well-being becomes apparently more salient in older age (most likely due to the higher prevalence

---

[15] In comparing the coefficients across data sets it should be remembered that not in all the data sets did the index contain all the components (refer to tables for detail).

of health problems in that age group), an increasing impact of such problems with age appears overemphasized in the responses to the open-ended questions. Apparently, young people and particularly middle-aged people are as much affected by health problems, if they happen to be afflicted, as are older people.

Also consistently weak is the impact of satisfaction with residence which often includes satisfaction with housing as well as with community. However, this finding is consistent with the low numbers of mentions of housing as a source of happiness in response to the open-ended question.

Summary and Discussion

Again, in this chapter, focusing on the impact of subjective assessment of major roles and resources on subjective well-being, we find little evidence for differential effects by age. Although there is a tendency for a more substantial impact of leisure and interpersonal satisfactions among older respondents but less impact of work and marital satisfactions for this age group, the differences are small and not entirely consistent across data sets. These findings reinforce our earlier conclusions that the prediction of overall subjective well-being does not seem to follow different mechanisms at different age levels.

Unlike in the findings of the previous chapter, the coefficients for specific predictors are not very consistent across data sets. We suspect that the inconsistency is at least partly due to a multicollinearity problem: Satisfactions with various life domains are quite substantially interrelated. Although, we combined the most highly interrelated variables into indices, even these indices remain interrelated. And substantial multicollinearity affects the reliability of the estimates as well as the size of the effects.

It is also worth noting that despite the inconsistency of the single coefficients, the amount of variance accounted for by all domain satisfactions is quite consistent across data sets. The set of domain satisfactions investigated here accounts for 40 to 50 percent of the variance in life satisfaction measures and for 25 to 35 percent of the variance in happiness measures.

This latter finding suggests that an index based on satisfactions with the major life domains could serve as a measure of general life satisfaction. Such a measure would even have an advantage over the one-question life satisfaction measure: It would be more reliable since it would be based on several single questions.

Table 6-1

Quality of Life Survey, 1978: Multiple Regressions,
Predicting Life Satisfaction and Happiness from
Domain Satisfactions and Age x Dom. Sat. Interactions

Predictors:	Life Satisfaction			Happiness		
	25-44	45-64	65-97	25-44	45-64	65-97
Economic Satisfaction	.177[c]	.167[b]	.297[a]* .347	.045[a]	.222[b]	.045[a]* .058
Residence Satisfaction	.061[c]	.005[b]	.148[a]* .137	.052[a]	.052[a]	.052[a]* .053
Job Satisfaction	.023[c]	.240[b]	.126[a]* .143	.180[a]	-.136[b]	.180[a]* .223
Health Satisfaction	.106[a]	.106[a]	.106[a]* .132	.095[b]	.011[a]	.011[a] .016
Marriage Satisfaction	.187[a]	.187[a]	.187[a]* .175	.327[c]	.069[b]	-.039[a] -.041
Interpersonal/Leisure Satisfaction	.380[a]	.380[a]	.380[a]* .310	.124[b]	.321[a]	.321[a]* .288
R^2, adj.		.478			.283	

Note: For each predictor, entries in the first line are unstandardized regression coefficients, entries in the second line (for the oldest group) are standardized regression coefficients. Identical superscripts of coefficients across age levels mean that the respective interaction term is not significant at the .05 level. Thus, the presence of a 'b' or 'c' superscript indicates that the interaction term for that age group was significantly different from that of the 65-97 age group at the .05 level.

High scores mean high satisfaction or happiness.

* p<.05

Table 6-2

Quality of Life Survey, 1971: Multiple Regressions,
Predicting Life Satisfaction and Happiness from
Domain Satisfactions and Age x Dom. Sat. Interactions

Predictors:	Life Satisfaction			Happiness		
	25-44	45-64	65-97	25-44	45-64	65-97
Economic Satisfaction	.218^a	.218^a	.218^a* / .233	.124^b	.231^a	.231^a* / .263
Residence Satisfaction	-.010^a	.145^b	-.010^a / -.010	.032^a	.032^a	.032^a / .035
Job Satisfaction	.266^c	.134^b	.082^a / .092	.280^b	-.146^a	-.146^a* / -.174
Health satisfaction	.008^a	.147^b	.008^a / .010	-.003^a	.136^b	-.003^a / -.004
Marriage satisfaction	.218^b	.100^a	.100^a* / .089	.383^b	.065^a	.065^a / .061
Interpersonal/leisure Satisfaction	.305^b	.498^a	.498^a* / .411	.068^a	.335^b	.068^a / .060
R^2, adj.		.461			.315	

Note: For each predictor, entries in the first line are unstandardized regression coefficients, entries in the second line ((for the oldest group) are standardized regression coefficients. Identical superscript of coefficients across age levels mean that the respective interaction term is not significant at the .05 level. Thus, the presence of a 'b' or 'c' superscript indicates that the interaction term for that age group was significantly different from that of the 65-97 age group at the .05 level.

High scores mean high satisfaction or happiness.

* p<.05

Table 6-3

Social Indicator Survey, 1972: Multiple Regressions,
Predicting Life Satisfaction and Happiness from
Domain Satisfactions and Age x Dom. Sat. Interactions

	Life Satisfaction			Happiness		
	25-44	45-64	65-97	25-44	45-64	65-97
Predictors:						
Economic Satisfaction	$.189^a$	$.189^a$	$.189^a$* / .208	$.118^c$	$.222^b$	$.365^a$* / .353
Residence Satisfaction	$.120^c$	$.292^b$	$.000^a$ / .000	$.088^a$	$.088^a$	$.088^a$* / .076
Job Satisfaction	$.404^c$	$-.424^b$	$.000^a$ / .000	$.222^b$	$.000^a$	$.000^a$ / .000
Health Satisfaction	$.091^a$	$.091^a$	$.091^a$* / .127	$.097^a$	$.170^b$	$.097^a$* / .118
Marriage Satisfaction	$.343^a$	$.045^b$	$.343^a$* / .389	$.215^b$	$.098^a$	$.098^a$* / .098
Interpersonal/Leisure Satisfaction	$-.134^b$	$.495^a$	$.495^a$* / .384	$.113^a$	$.299^b$	$.113^a$* / .077
R^2, adj.		.438			.289	

Note: For each predictor, entries in the first line are unstandardized regression coefficients, entries in the second line (for the oldest group) are standardized regression coefficients. Identical superscript of coefficients across age levels mean that the respective interaction term is not significant at the .05 level. Thus, the presence of a 'b' or 'c' superscript indicates that the interaction term for that age group was significantly different from that of the 65-97 age group at the .05 level.

High scores mean high satisfaction or happiness.

* $p < .05$

Table 6-4

General Social Surveys, 1972-1978: Multiple
Regressions, Predicting Happiness from Domain
Satisfactions and Age x Dom. Sat. Interactions

	Happiness		
	25-44	45-64	65-97
Predictors:			
Economic Satisfaction	.230[a]	.316[b]	.230[a]*
			.131
Residence Satisfaction	.080[a]	.080[a]	.080[a]*
			.092
Job Satisfaction	.223[a]	.041[b]	.223[a]*
			.131
Health Satisfaction	.096[a]	.096[a]	.096[a]*
			.113
Marriage Satisfaction	1.147[c]	.497[b]	.625[a]*
			.259
Interpersonal/leisure Satisfaction	.126[a]	.226[b]	.126[a]*
			.102
R^2 adj.		.344	

Note: For each predictor, entries in the first line are unstandardized
regression coefficients, entries in the second line (for the oldest
group) are standardized regression coefficients. Identical
superscripts of coefficients across age levels mean that the
respective interaction term is not significant at the .05 level.
Thus, the presence of a 'b' or 'c' superscript indicates that the
interaction term for that age group was significantly different from
that of the 65-97 age group at the .05 level.

High scores mean high satisfaction or happiness.

* $p < .05$

Table 6-5

Detroit Social Indicator Study, 1973-74: Multiple Regressions,
Predicting Life Satisfaction and Happiness from
Domain Satisfactions and Age x Dom. Sat. Interactions

Predictors:	Life Satisfaction			Happiness		
	25-44	45-64	65-97	25-44	45-64	65-97
Economic Satisfaction	.204^c	.291^b	-.004^a -.004	.229^a	.229^a	.229^a* .280
Residence Satisfaction	.057^a	.057^a	.057^a* .060	.059^a	-.047^b	.059^a* .070
Job Satisfaction	.256^a	-.022^b	.256^a* .289	.013^a	.013^a	.013^a .016
Health Satisfaction	.206^b	.092^a	.092^a* .103	.070^a	.070^a	.070^a* .087
Marriage Satisfaction	.209^a	.209^a	.209^a* .142	.116^a	.116^a	.116^a* .088
Interpersonal/Leisure Satisfaction	.160^c	.264^b	.547^a* .517	.221^a	.221^a	.221^a .235
R^2 adj.		.444			.276	

Note: For each predictor, entries in the first line are unstandardized regression coefficients, entries in the
second line (for the oldest group) are standardized regression coefficients. Identical superscripts of
coefficients across age levels mean that the respective interaction term is not significant at the .05
level. Thus, the presence of a 'b' or 'c' superscript indicates that the interaction term for that age
group was significantly different from that of the 65-97 age group at the .05 level.

High scores mean high satisfaction or happiness.

* p<.05

CHAPTER 7

RETIRED WOMEN AND MEN: ACTIVITIES AND SUBJECTIVE WELL-BEING

Men and an increasingly large number of women spend much of their lives in work outside the home. Such work usually provides the basis of economic livelihood and constitutes one of the major roles of adult life. Thus, it is not surprising that retirement, the institutionalized termination of the work role, is often considered one of the most crucial events in the later part of life, disrupting many longstanding activity patterns and thereby creating traumatic effects.

However, available evidence suggests that the effects of retirement are actually less traumatic than commonly assumed. In several studies where the subjective well-being of working older adults was compared with that of retired elderly (Fox, 1977; Jaslow, 1976; Thompson, 1973; Chapter 5 of this report) it was found that retirement had little effect when such variables as income, health, or age were controlled. Streib and Schneider (1971) confirmed this basic conclusion with longitudinal data. In other words, it appears that older adults adjust on the average quite successfully to the loss of the work role.

Three theoretical propositions have been advanced to explain this adjustment process (see Atchley, 1976, for a review). One such proposition adopted by Friedman and Havighurst (1954) and Miller (1965) holds that in order to maintain a pre-retirement level of subjective well-being, activities or roles must be found that can substitute for work activities as a source of personal fulfillment. Another proposition (Atchley, 1972) focuses on modification rather than change, postulating that expansion of existing roles and activities rather than the assumption of new ones facilitates adjustment to the loss of work and promotes well-being. In contrast to these two theoretical statements which predict subjective well-being to be positively related to maintenance of activity levels, the theory of disengagement (Cumming & Henry, 1961) postulates that the gradual withdrawal from activities is actually necessary to allow the aging individual to maintain his or her well-being. According to disengagement theory, the empirical relationship between subjective well-being and activity level ought to be negative. While none of these propositions speaks specifically to the relationship between activities and well-being for the pre-retirement stage, it is assumed in this chapter that certain activities which did not serve any such function before retirement may emerge as new sources of subjective well-being after retirement. This means that any activity could conceivably be related to well-being among the retired but not among the working older adults.

Little is known about the effect of retirement on the entire set of individual activities and roles. Obviously, most work-related activities are

73

terminated at the point of retirement; but how does this change affect a retiring individual's entire life style? It is commonly assumed that work-related activities are simply replaced by passive leisure past-times such as reading, watching television programs, and the like; but it may be the case that daily routines such as homemaking, maintenance and personal care are expanded after retirement, consuming much of the extra free time (Lowenthal & Robinson, 1976). Or lost contacts with coworkers may be replaced by increased social activities (Cottrell & Atchley, 1969; Lowenthal & Robinson, 1976). And finally, involvement in volunteer work and in formal organizations may be sought to compensate for the loss of the work role and its attendant feelings of useful involvement (Streib & Schneider, 1971). Evidence available on the last two hypotheses (Cottrell & Atchley, 1969; Palmore & Luikart, 1972) suggests that levels of participation in social or organizational activities are the same or higher for the retired older adults than for the older adults who are still working.

With regard to the effect of activities on subjective well-being, a much larger body of data is available as a result of the continued interest in adjustment to older age. Overall, a positive relationship between subjective well-being and the level of various social (Larson, 1978) or non-social activities (Maddox, 1963; Sauer, 1977) is indicated, although the relationship is frequently quite weak and is weakened even further when socioeconomic and health statuses are controlled (Bull & Aucoin, 1975; Conner, Powers & Bultena, 1979; Cutler, 1973; George, 1978; Palmore & Luikart, 1972).

Pursuing the theoretical propositions discussed above, this chapter explores two issues: (1) How do activities of retirees differ in terms of content and duration from activities of older people who are still working? (2) Do some activities provide sources of well-being for the retirees, balancing out the loss of work? Activities are measured by the time-budget method, which asks respondents to report the succession of activities they engage in over the course of a 24-hour day. This allows a more comprehensive and objective assessment of the extent of daily activities than traditional measurement devices which typically ask only about a few select activities using rather general response scales (for example, a scale ranging from "daily" to "yearly").

Method

Respondents

The present analysis is based on respondents 50 years old and older drawn from a probability sample of American adults living in the coterminous United States. The original study was conducted by the Survey Research Center of The University of Michigan under the title "Time Use in Economic and Social Accounts" (Principal Investigators: F.T. Juster, P. Courant, G.J. Duncan, J.P. Robinson, F.P. Stafford). The cross section was interviewed in October and November 1975. Complete data were available on 410 respondents, including 125 working men, 113 retired men, 91 working women, and 81 retired women.

Design

Differences in activity patterns between retired and working older adults were investigated by comparing reported activities. The relationship of these activities with life satisfaction in retirement was explored by examining the interrelationship between each activity and life satisfaction among the retired respondents. Self-reported health, family income and age were statistically controlled in these analyses in order to eliminate the most obvious alternative explanations of observed effects--worse health, lower income and higher age among the retired and less active than among the working and more active older adults. The investigations were carried out separately for men and women, since patterns were expected to differ by sex.

Measures

Activities were measured by a diary method, whereby respondents reported each activity for the entire 24-hour period prior to the interview, starting at midnight.[16] Reported activities were coded into a set of approximately 100 categories which can be grouped as follows: (1) work and work-related activities; (2) household activities, such as cooking, cleaning, gardening, and repairs around the house; (3) child care; (4) activities related to obtaining goods and services, such as shopping; (5) personal care, including sleeping and napping; (6) education-related activities; (7) participation in various organizations such as clubs, church, etc.; (8) social relations and entertainment, such as visiting with others, going to a movie or a sports event; (9) active leisure, such as playing games, going for a walk, and doing crafts; (10) passive leisure, such as watching television programs, reading and writing.

Two types of measures were used for the analyses (Stone, 1972). The first can be understood as denoting simple participation. As such it indicates whether a respondent reports having engaged at all in a particular type of activity during the previous day. Activities of a very common nature such as sleeping were reported by 100 percent of the respondents, while a more specific activity such as participation in voluntary associations was reported by only about 20 percent of all the respondents. A second measure refers to duration; it measures the actual time spent by the respondents on any given type of activity. For example, the overall average time spent by all retired men on voluntary associations was about 24 minutes, while the overall average time spent by retired women was about 36 minutes.

Work status was operationalized as "working" and "retired." Respondents

---

[16] Although we recognized the desirability of repeated measurement to tone down fluctuations associated with the day of the week and the season, it was not feasible to analyze data from four waves of interviewing conducted in the Time Use study over the span of one year: due to panel attrition the number of adults over 50 who completed all four waves was very small. Nevertheless, we performed identical analyses on the total time of respondents who answered all four waves, and found the patterns to be quite similar although less likely to be significant due to small numbers of cases.

were classified as working if they labeled themselves as such in a question
about their work status or if they reported in a subsequent question that they
were doing any work for pay at the present time. They were classified as
retired if they labeled themselves as such and did not report any work at all.
Respondents who labeled themselves as housewives were excluded because of the
irrelevance of formal retirement for that group.[17] Health status was measured
by a question probing personal health in relation to that of others of the
same age and providing the four response alternatives "excellent," "good,"
"fair," and "poor." Age was measured in years. Family income was assessed by
a closed-ended question providing 18 income brackets on a show card; for
analysis purpose midpoint dollar amounts were assigned to each bracket.
Finally, satisfaction with life was measured on a 7-point Likert-type response
scale ranging from "terrible" to "delighted" to the question "How do you feel
about your life as a whole?"

Data analysis

For comparing retired and working older adults with regard to activity
categories a set of multiple regression analyses were conducted separately for
men and women, in each of which one activity category was regressed on
employment status, self-reported health, family income and age.

Another set of multiple regression analyses was utilized to investigate
the effect of activity categories on life satisfaction. In each regression
analysis life satisfaction was regressed on one type of activity plus self-
reported health, family income and age. The analyses were conducted
separately for retired men, retired women, working men, and working women,
since as noted above the effects of activities on well-being were expected to
differ for retired and working older adults.

Findings

Effect of retirement on patterns of activities

In this section the effect of retirement on the categories of activities
are explored separately for men and women. Table 7-1 shows the unadjusted
percentages of respondents who report any participation in each of the various
activities, while Table 7-2 shows the unadjusted number of minutes spent in
each activity. Unstandardized coefficients indicate the strength of the

---

[17] Responses to a set of questions on work history indicate that even from
the women who label themselves as housewives only 25 percent never worked
full-time at all. But these women do on the average report a smaller mean
number of years spent in the work force--10.9 years full-time and 2.2 years
part-time--than the women who label themselves as retired. The retired women
report a mean of 28 years full-time and 5.9 years part-time work. Moreover,
only two of the retired women do not report any full-time work at all; but one
of them reports 40 years part-time.

retirement effect when controlling on self-reported health, family income, and age.[18]

The figures on work-related activities in Tables 7-1 and 7-2 demonstrate clearly that the classification of work status was successful in separating retired older people from older people who were still working; i.e., practically no retired respondents reported that they had been working on the previous day and average time spent in work-related activities is very much lower among this group than among the working respondents.[19]

As shown in Table 7-1, the rate of participation by older women in social and entertainment-related activities is substantially higher after retirement, largely because a higher percentage of them visit with others, as shown in data which are not reported here. The overall difference is statistically significant (p < .01) when the effects of health, age and family income are controlled. Among older men, the participation rate in social entertainment activities is slightly but not significantly higher for retired men. Instead, retired men engage more frequently in active leisure pursuits, particularly outdoor activities; the difference is significant (p < .05). Another significant difference in participation rate among men is observed for activities related to obtaining goods and services (p < .05). Otherwise, no major differences between retired and working older adults emerge. More specifically, retired respondents do not participate in higher numbers in organizational and child care activities (they also do not participate in higher numbers in personal care, household and passive leisure activities, although the latter results cannot be interpreted since virtually all of the working older adults already engage in these activities to some extent and thus little or no increase in participation rate is possible).

Turning now to the figures on average time spent in various activities by working and retired men and women (Table 7-2), one major difference to Table 7-1 is immediately obvious: the time spent on passive leisure activities is considerably greater among the retired of both sexes than among the working older adults, a difference which is statistically significant (p < .01). Actually, retired respondents spend about one third more time per day on passive leisure than do older respondents who are still working. (Data which are not presented here show that television viewing is a major component of this category.)

However, we must note that the difference in results between the two tables is to be attributed to the different nature of the indices employed; i.e., since almost all of the working respondents report at least some passive leisure, a ceiling effect for participation rate is created, allowing no

---

[18] Unstandardized regression coefficients were used since the coefficients for effects of retirement were to be compared across several regression analyses.

[19] Since we report on activities that could refer to any day of the week, weekdays as well as weekend days, a proportion of the working respondents do not report any work activities; and those respondents presumably report more non-work activities than they would on a work-day. This fact is bound to cloud the comparisons somewhat.

further increase. On the other hand, the actual time that working older adults spend on passive leisure is obviously far from the maximum possible, allowing for considerable increase in reported time. In other words, the passive leisure role is not newly acquired after retirement but it is significantly expanded.

A similar situation is observed for household work: at least among women, almost everybody reports some housework for the previous day (Table 7-1), so that no substantial difference in participation due to retirement is possible. However, as shown in Table 7-2, women who are retired spend more time on household activities, a difference which is significant (p < .05). For men, a significant (p < .05) difference in time spent on housework (Table 7-2) is paralleled by a noticeable although not significant difference of participation for such activities (Table 7-1). Table 7-2 replicates the effect of retirement on social and entertainment-related activities among women as documented in Table 7-1; i.e. retired women spend more time in such activities, (p < .05). Finally, Table 7-2 shows that retired older adults do not differ significantly from working older adults with regard to the time they spend on personal care, organizational activities, active leisure and-- for men--social and service-related activities.

To summarize, two measures were used to test the effect of retirement on activity patterns. Examination of the first index--percentages of respondents who engage at all in a given activity--showed that retired women are more likely than working women to participate in social activities, and that retired men are more likely than working men to participate in active leisure pursuits and activities for obtaining goods and services. Analysis of the second index--average time spent in each activity--showed that retired women also spend more time than working women on social activities. A difference in the average time spent between the two groups may be due to two types of differences: Either different proportions of respondents participate or the same proportion participates but spends a different amount of time. In the case of women's social activities the former seems to be the case. Such an interpretation is confirmed by an examination of the average time spent by those women who report having participated at all in social activities (data not shown). Amongst them the average times are very similar for both retired and working. In addition, retired women as well as men spend more time on passive leisure and household activities than do their working counterparts. These differences, on the other hand, are not due to a higher number of participants, but rather to an expansion of the time already spent on the same activities when working, since almost everybody engages in some passive leisure and some housework before retirement.

In conclusion, retired women engage more often in social activities and retired men more often in active leisure than do their working counterparts. Also, retirees spend more time on passive leisure activities and, to a lesser extent, on housework. Of further interest is the fact that retired people are neither more likely to participate in organizational activities nor do they engage more extensively in personal care activities than working older adults.

Activities and life satisfaction

In order to detect any activities which may emerge as sources of
satisfaction after retirement, the relationships between activities and life
satisfaction were examined separately for employed and retired men and women.
Tables 7-3 and 7-4 show the zero-order correlations between life satisfaction
and the two types of indices. Also shown are the unstandardized and
standardized partial regression coefficients after controlling on self-
reported health, family income and age. The most striking feature of these
two tables is the general lack of significant relationships. A few
coefficients are statistically significant; but given the total number of
coefficients these could be due to mere chance and therefore do not warrant
much consideration. However, two types of activities which have negative or
weakly positive relationships among the working older adults emerge with
consistently positive although not always significant relationships among the
retired. These are organizational involvement for males and social and
entertainment activities for females.

In sum, the findings on the relationships between life satisfaction and
activities provide little support for the notion that engaging in any of the
investigated types of activities or the time spent on them improves overall
life satisfaction among the retired, although a tendency for increased
satisfaction to be associated with higher organizational activities in males
and with higher social activities in females is noticeable.

Summary and Discussion

The present chapter addresses itself to the observation, reported by
several authors and replicated in this report, that retirement has no
significant effect on overall subjective well-being among older respondents,
and explored specifically the role of activities by examining the following
issues: (1) How does the pattern of activities differ between retired and
working older Americans? (2) How do activities in retirement relate to overall
life satisfaction? These questions were studied by comparing working and
retired men and women over 50 years of age from a national probability sample
with regard to their participation and time spent in global activity
categories, and respective relationships between these activities and life
satisfaction.

When interpreting the findings, a number of caveats should be considered.
Since the study employed a cross-sectional design, neither actual change in
activity following retirement nor actual change in satisfaction after an
increase in activity can be directly demonstrated. The data can only be used
to show differences between employed and retired people or between people at
various levels of activity as they are at the point of data collection. To
the extent that alternative explanations can be excluded--such as variations
in income, age or health--differences can be attributed more confidently to a
change in employment status or in activity level. However, since other
alternative explanations can never be entirely discounted, such attributions
must be made with caution. Moreover, due to the cross-sectional nature of the
data the direction of causation remains uncertain. It has been assumed here

that the event of retirement modifies activity patterns, and that involvement in activities affects satisfaction; but it could also be argued that more active people are more likely to retire, and that more satisfied elderly are more likely to engage in all sorts of activities. The cross-sectional data upon which the present analyses were based do not allow us to distinguish between the various causal sequences.

In this chapter the previously reported lack of effect of employment status on subjective well-being was replicated; the standardized regression coefficient was $\beta = .00$ for males and $\beta = .00$ for females, after income, age, and self-reported health were controlled. With regard to the first issue-- effect of retirement on the patterns of activities--it was shown that retired older adults spend a significantly larger amount of time on passive leisure and on housework activities than working older adults; retired men are also somewhat more likely to engage in active leisure and service-related activities and retired women in social activities. More generally, these findings suggest that the time released from work responsibilities is primarily invested in passive leisure, and, to a lesser degree, in housework and--for females--in social activities. With respect to the hypotheses formulated at the outset of this chapter, this implies that passive leisure and some maintenance-related activities are more clearly replacing work activities among retirees than are the types of activities commonly considered important for maintaining an active involvement in later life, such as organizational and social activities. Although slight increases in these latter activities are indicated, they reach marginal statistical significance at best. The data therefore support the notion of a certain decline in social and productive activities after retirement, and are thus consistent with disengagement theory as far as it refers to a withdrawal from active pastimes.

With regard to the second issue, the present results do not indicate any types of activities as new sources of satisfaction after retirement; this negative finding holds for the participation rate as well as the actual time spent in these activities. Although a few types of activities show stronger positive relationships with life satisfaction among the retirees than among the workers, the relationships are largely non-significant.

This virtual lack of significant positive relationships between activities and life satisfaction casts doubt on the validity of the relationships as reported elsewhere and adds credibility to studies questioning their existence. In particular the finding raises questions about the importance of the quantitative aspects of activities. Various authors (e.g., Conner, Powers, & Bultena, 1979; Lowenthal & Robinson, 1976) have in fact suggested that the quality of social contacts may be more critical for maintaining high morale in older age than participation rate and duration. For example, Lowenthal and Haven (1968) have shown that the sole availability of a close confidante contributes significantly to the morale of older people, irrespective of the frequency of the interaction with the confidante. By the same token, the qualitative dimension of other activities may be crucial in evaluating their effects.

In conclusion, the present study confirms previous reports indicating little difference in subjective well-being between retired and still working older adults. The analysis shows however that this lack of difference cannot be explained in terms of activities. Retired older adults do spend more time

on passive leisure and housework than working older adults; and more older
retired men engage in active leisure than working men, while more retired
older women engage in social activities than working older women. None of
these activities, however, relates clearly to life satisfaction. Thus, our
findings lend little support to any of the theoretical propositions raised in
the beginning of this chapter, each of which postulates either a positive or a
negative correlation between life satisfaction and activity level.

Table 7-1

Unadjusted Percentages of Respondents Participating
in Each Type of Activity During
the Previous Day

	Working males (N=125)	Retired males (N=113)	B-coeff., controlling on health, family income, and age	Working females (N=91)	Retired females (N=81)	B-coeff., controlling on health, family income, and age
Work	69%	4%	-.55**	68%	5%	-.56**
Household	59%	77%	.18	92%	96%	.03
Child care	9%	7%	.02	11%	10%	.08
Services	44%	50%	.25*	52%	43%	.07
Personal care	100%	100%	--	100%	100%	--
Education	2%	1%	.00	1%	4%	.05
Organizations	16%	16%	-.04	23%	24%	-.02
Social/Entertainment	25%	32%	.03	34%	59%	.33**
Active leisure	16%	38%	.20*	28%	35%	.07
Passive leisure	94%	96%	.00	93%	96%	.07

* $p < .05$,   ** $p < .01$

p.43, third paragraph, 7th line, should read:

... age are r = -.37 and r = -.34 in the two surveys.

p.43, third paragraph, 10th and 11th lines, should read:

... (r = -.26 and r = -.14). These effects are further registered by the older respondents ...

p.47, in Table 4-1, second to last column, third coefficient from bottom, should read:

-.04

p.47, in Table 4-1, second to last column, the bottom coefficient is lacking; it should read:

.06

p.47, in Table 4-1, third to last column, 3rd coefficient from bottom (.05)

Note: this coefficient should be marked with an asterisk for significance.

p.47, in Table 4-1, 4th to last column, 6th coefficient from bottom (.05*)

Note: this coefficient should not be marked with an asterisk.

p.54, last line, should read:

... respondents. Young blacks report less happiness than young whites; less ...

p.56-61, p.68-72, footnote, last sentence, should read:

Thus, the presence of a 'b' or 'c' superscript indicates that the regression coefficient for that age group was significantly different from that of the 65-97 age group at the .05 level.

p.65, third paragraph, should read:

The impact of economic satisfaction shows little systematic variation by age. That is, in some data sets a similar coefficient adequately describes the effect of economic satisfaction for all age groups; and in the data sets where this is not true, the variation by age is inconsistent. The lack of systematic age variation suggests that the subjective quality of economic conditions is not of differential importance for older, middle-aged, and young Americans' overall subjective well-being. This finding is quite consistent with the results to the open-ended questions discussed above; i.e., not only is economic satisfaction important at any age level, but for respondents of

Subjective Well-Being Among Different Age Groups, 1982

p.13

Note: The number of respondents in the 1976 study by Veroff et al. was 2264.

p.19-21, Tables 2-1 through 2-3

Note: Chi-square values have been included for all mentioned "reasons" although for some "reasons" expected cell frequencies include frequencies below 5. These Chi-square values should have been indicated in the tables such that they can be evaluated with proper caution. They include:

Table 2-1: other relatives' situation.

Table 2-2: spouse, general; children, general; lack of children; respondent's future health; respondent's future material resources; respondent's independence; spiritual; and other.

Table 2-3: spouse, general; lack of spouse; respondent's relationship with spouse; non-relatives' situation; other economic worries; personal situation, general; spiritual; and other.

p.21, Table 2-3

The Chi-square value for the "worry always" category is incorrect; it should read:

18.41**.

p.21, Table 2-3

For the category "Respondent's future health," asterisks are placed incorrectly: Asterisks should be included for 20-29, 30-39, 40-49, 60-69, 70-79, 80++, but not for 50-59 and Total.

For the category "Personal situation, general," asterisks are placed incorrectly: they should be included for 20-29 but not for Total.

p.35, footnote, the following sentence should be added:

The major modification concerns a slight shortening of the age range from 20 through 90 to 25 through 90.

p.41, third paragraph, 12th and 13th lines, should read:

... correlation coefficients range from .10 to .14).

3

all ages this particular source is among the most frequently
mentioned reasons for happiness, unhappiness, and worries.

p.66, parenthesis in footnote, should read:

(refer to Appendix A for details)

p.72, last column, bottom coefficient (.221)

Note: This coefficient should be marked with an asterisk for
significance.

p.84-85, Tables 7-3 and 7-4, footnote, should read:

... unstandardized (B) and standardized (β) regression
coefficients, regressing life satisfaction on participation in
activity category plus control variables (i.e., self-reported
health, family income, and age). Higher scores ...

Table 7-2

Unadjusted Mean Number of Minutes Spent on Each Type
of Activity During the Previous Day

	Working males (N=125)	Retired males (N=113)	B-coeff., controlling on health, family income, and age	Working females (N=91)	Retired females (N=81)	B-coeff., controlling on health, family income, and age
Work	350.8	6.5	-278.3**	299.5	9.6	-239.9**
Household	71.4	137.2	71.4*	135.1	171.2	84.1*
Child care	6.9	9.8	10.4	12.6	15.7	13.3
Services	42.6	47.0	19.5	48.5	58.7	36.2*
Personal care	660.2	759.2	35.5	672.1	740.2	13.1
Education	5.0	.9	0.2	2.1	5.8	8.7
Organizations	24.2	24.1	-0.1	22.2	35.8	13.3
Social/Entertainment	40.2	49.5	-2.9	40.9	80.8	50.6*
Active leisure	26.7	62.0	25.5	36.5	45.6	14.7
Passive leisure	211.7	343.8	136.0**	170.6	276.7	123.1**

* p<.05.   ** p<.01

Table 7-3

Relationship Between Participation in Activity
and Life Satisfaction

	Working males (N=125)			Retired males (N=113)			Working females (N=91)			Retired females (N=81)		
	r	β	B	r	β	B	r	β	B	r	β	B
Work	.16	.12	.26	.12	.06	.49	-.08	-.11	-.26	-.03	-.01	-.09
Household	-.11	-.08	-.16	-.14	-.14	-.42	-.04	-.11	-.49	.19	.21	1.42
Child care	-.12	-.16	-.40	-.19	-.09	-.51	.12	.12	.48	-.01	.06	.25
Services	-.10	-.12	-.21	.00	-.13	-.32	-.12	-.13	-.27	.05	.06	.15
Personal care	--	--	--	--	--	--	--	--	--	--	--	--
Education	-.04	-.07	-.43	-.02	-.03	-.42	--	--	--	.08	.12	.83
Organizations	-.12	-.14	-.31	.19	.14	.54	.06	.04	.10	-.04	-.06	-.18
Social/Entertainment	-.11	-.07	-.15	-.15	-.10	-.29	.00	-.01	.02	.17	.14	.31
Active leisure	.02	.02	-.02	-.04	-.04	-.06	-.07	-.12	-.28	-.01	.00	.02
Passive leisure	-.03	.02	.11	.04	-.02	-.17	-.04	-.06	-.24	.22	.20	1.29

Note: Entries are zero-order correlation coefficients (r) between life satisfaction and participation in activity category and unstandardized (B) and standardized (β) regression coefficients, regressing participation in activity category, self-reported health, family income and age on life satisfaction. Higher scores indicate higher satisfaction with life.

* p<.05, ** p<.01

Table 7-4

Relationship Between Time Spent in Activity
and Life Satisfactions

	Working males (N=125)			Retired males (N=113)			Working females (N=91)			Retired females (N=81)		
	r	β	B	r	β	B	r	β	B	r	β	B
Work	.12	.08	.0003	.15	.10	.0032	-.02	-.02	.0000	.02	.04	.0010
Household	-.25*	-.23*	-.0020*	.01	.04	.0002	.17	.16	.0015	-.02	.00	-.0001
Child care	-.09	-.15	-.0042	-.21	-.21	-.0058	-.03	.04	-.0008	-.12	-.05	-.0009
Services	-.07	-.07	-.0008	-.07	-.17	-.0030	-.12	-.13	-.0018	.01	.00	.0002
Personal care	.00	-.02	-.0001	-.03	.03	.0002	-.05	-.04	-.0003	-.19	-.18	-.0014
Education	-.07	-.11	-.0029	-.02	.03	-.0040	--	--	--	.08	.12	.0031
Organizations	-.10	-.11	-.0011	.27*	.24*	.0046*	-.01	-.02	-.0005	.01	-.01	-.0002
Social/Entertainment	-.09	-.06	-.0007	-.19	-.13	-.0019	.05	.09	.0013	.30*	.26	.0030
Active leisure	.08	.11	.0008	.12	.06	.0006	-.07	-.06	-.0007	.07	.07	.0011
Passive leisure	.11	.16	.0011	-.03	-.04	-.0002	.08	.06	.0005	-.02	-.04	-.0003

Note: Entries are zero-order correlation coefficients (r) between life satisfaction and time
spent in activity category, and unstandardized (B) and standardized (β) regression
coefficients, regressing time spent in activity category, self-reported health, family
income, and age on life satisfaction.

* p<.05, ** p<.01

CHAPTER 8

SUMMARY AND CONCLUSION

In this report we set out to find answers to a number of questions revolving around the relationship of age and subjective well-being, an issue not heretofore extensively explored in either the quality of life or the gerontological literature. Data from several surveys of the American adult population were used in our investigation. By replicating our analysis on a number of different datasets wherever possible, we sought to focus our attention on robust findings and to justify more confidence in our conclusions than would be warranted if they were based on data from a single survey.

Following are brief summaries of some of our more significant findings along with the questions we sought to answer.

Do various age groups share a common understanding of subjective well-being? Perhaps the first question--before any structured investigations of subjective well-being are attempted--should explore how people describe their subjective well-being in their own words. When people were asked directly about what made them happy, what made them unhappy, and what made them worried, persons of all age groups described their economic situation as an important source of well-being (Chapter 2). Likewise, all age groups viewed their children as an important source of happiness. On the other hand, older people differed from other age groups in that they were more likely to cite their health as a source of happiness, unhappiness, and worries. While proportions of persons who are married or employed decline among older age levels, this cannot account for the entire decline in mentions of these domains as sources of subjective well-being. Apparently, some of the decline represents a turning away from these domains, probably in preparation for their eventual loss. In general, however, these observed shifts in perceived sources of well-being across age groups are consistent with the age patterns of major roles and responsibilities across the life span.

Other findings that emerged from our analysis of what people said made them happy--and that were not consistent with suggestions in the literature-- were that hobbies, spare time activities, and independence of their personal situation did not figure prominently as perceived sources of happiness or unhappiness for older people. Although older respondents did mention leisure activities at slightly higher rates than younger respondents, this source does not emerge with high frequency in the older age group and thus does not present itself as a major alternative source replacing spouse and work as sources of well-being.

Of course, people's own perceptions of what lies at the core of their happiness is only one way of investigating the personal understanding of subjective well-being. We also examined the meaning of subjective well-being from a different angle by using a different set of measures.

Does a similar structure of dimensions of subjective well-being tend to emerge across all age groups? A different way of assessing the meaning of subjective well-being is represented by unravelling the dimensions of the conceptual space that individuals use when they mark standardized rating scales of subjective well-being in various domains of life. The technique traditionally associated with such an approach is factor analysis. After noting the shortcomings of previous research in which factor analysis was performed for different age groups, we used what we believed was a more appropriate factor analytical approach to explore the dimensions of subjective well-being in different age groups (Chapter 3). We found that four factors best represented the dimensions underlying subjective well-being in various life domains for all individuals from 25 to 74 years of age. These four factors were (1) health; (2) economic situation; (3) residential environment; and (4) spare time activities, family, and friends.

Persons aged 18 to 24 had factors that were significantly different; and there were too few people 75 years or older to make any definitive statements about the factor structure amongst this age group. In conclusion, we can say that similar factors nicely represents the patterning of subjective well-being elements across the 25 to 74 age group.

How is age related to subjective well-being and how might we account for this relationship? Our finding that older people tended to report a higher level of satisfaction further confirmed the findings of other researchers (Chapter 4). However, we went beyond merely asking about the relationship of subjective well-being to age and sought to explain it through a combination of several types of explanations. Three factors related to subjective adjustment processes--religiosity, social desirability, and increased familiarity producing greater liking--accounted for a significant portion of the effect of age. Among indicators of objective improvement, a decrease in the number of presumably stressful life events and freedom from obligations accounted for another portion of the increased life satisfaction amongst older persons. Certain other variables associated with the objective situation--health, education, income--actually suppressed the relationship between age and life satisfaction such that when we controlled for these variables, the relationship was stronger than without controls.

Do factors, measuring occupancy of various roles and differential access to resources, have different effects on subjective well-being across various age groups? Our findings were quite consistent and show the following patterns (Chapter 5). Among the factors examined while holding all other factors constant, marital status (being married) had the strongest effect on subjective well-being, displaying a similarly strong effect across all age groups. Good health also had a strong effect. However, unlike in some of the previous studies, good health did not have a stronger effect among the older respondents than among other age groups. Income and education displayed effects too inconsistent to produce any interpretable pattern. Finally, sex and employment status showed little effect at any age level. The only factor that had a differential impact at different age levels was race--with being Black significantly depressing happiness among the youngest age group but not among the other age groups.

In sum, from among the factors investigated here the resource factors of being married and in good health have a positive impact on subjective well-being, other factors being equal. Moreover, the impact of these two factors is quite general, being evident at all age levels and on subjective well-being conceptualized both as life satisfaction and as happiness.

Is satisfaction with various aspects of life related differently to general subjective well-being across various age groups? Affecting the old as well as other age groups at similar strength, satisfaction with financial situation turned out to be the specific domain satisfaction having the most powerful impact on subjective well-being when all other domain satisfactions were controlled (Chapter 6). Perhaps an even more notable finding is that health satisfaction has little impact on the subjective well-being of the older age group despite many suggestions in the literature and previous research evidence indicating that this is an important determinant of subjective well-being for older people.

Some domain satisfactions have a differential impact on overall well-being in different age groups. These age patterns were generally consistent with the differential saliency of the domains for different age levels. Thus, marriage and work satisfactions were generally less important for overall subjective well-being among the older than the younger age groups, while an index which combined interpersonal and leisure satisfactions was somewhat more important among older than younger age groups.

The findings from this set of analyses were somewhat less consistent across data sets than the findings on the impact of sociodemographic factors on subjective well-being. For example, while residential and job satisfactions were significant predictors for certain age groups and in some datasets, they either displayed a different age pattern or were not statistically significant in other datasets. We believe that the inconsistency is at least partly caused by the statistical properties of the relevant data. I.e., the satisfactions with specific domains of life that we used as predictors of general subjective well-being were quite highly interrelated, thereby modifying the reliability of the regression coefficients. An appropriate strategy for dealing with interrelated predictors is to form indices out of the most highly interrelated variables. Thus, we formed the following indices: index of leisure and interpersonal satisfactions, index of residential satisfactions, index of economic satisfaction. However, not even this procedure was able to eliminate the problem entirely.

How do older people who still work compare with retired older people in terms of patterning of activities and relationship of activities to life satisfaction? Since our analyses showed consistently little difference in happiness and life satisfaction between retired and still working older people when other factors were controlled, we sought to find why this pattern occurs (Chapter 7). Neither of our three hypotheses (substitution of activities; expansion of activities; and reduction in activity roles) were supported by our analysis. In fact, the pattern of activities of retired older adults differed little from those older adults who are still working, with the exception that retired women were more likely to participate in social activities, retired men more likely to participate in active leisure and obtaining goods and services, and that both sexes spent more time on passive leisure such as TV watching and on house work when retired. Moreover, with the possible exceptions of the time spent in organizational activities by men

and the time spent in social/entertainment activities by women, neither the
participation in activities nor the time spent in activities had any
significant effect on level of subjective well-being amongst retired older
people.

In the following paragraphs we will attempt to integrate these findings
under a few general issues that we raised at the outset of this investigation.

Overall age differences. Although older adults think spontaneously of
some different reasons why they are happy or worried than younger adults--more
often of health, less often of work and marriage--certain other reasons such
as economic concerns or children are common to both age groups. Moreover, the
meaning of life satisfaction as revealed in the patterning of standardized
ratings of domain satisfactions is quite stable across the age range of 25
through 74.

Based on these findings, we feel justified in utilizing satisfaction
measures for cross-age comparisons of subjective well-being and its
predictors. In other words, we believe that the differences in subjective
well-being that we observed for different age levels do not just represent an
artifact of differential meaning of the concept and/or its measures. The
stability of sociodemographic predictor patterns across age levels further
underscores the robustness of the concept of global subjective well-being for
age comparisons.

As for the relationship between age and satisfactions we feel that more
work needs to be done on exploring whether the higher levels of subjective
well-being reported by older respondents reflect a true state of affairs or,
at least partly, a defensive or adaptive reporting. If the observed increase
in satisfaction is partly attributable to the differential operation of social
desirability, this would suggest lower validity of satisfactions reported by
the elderly. If true, this has quite general implications for the measurement
of subjective well-being among older respondents.

Findings reported in the literature provide additional evidence that
responses by older respondents may be more influenced by factors other than
the true state of well-being and therefore may not be equally valid as those
by younger respondents. For example, Kogan (1961) and Gergen and Back (1967)
found that older respondents are more likely to use specific categories of
the response scale, such as the "agree" category, the extreme categories, and
the non-committal middle category.

While these tendencies reflect a set way of responding which is likely to
occur across all types of questions, some other evidence suggests that
defensive or adaptive processes involved here are more specific to the
reporting of satisfactions and subjective well-being. For example, Carp and
Carp (1981) note that older respondents show little inclination to complain
about any aspect of their housing until they are told that they have a chance
to move into better housing, at which point they produce numerous complaints.
Carp and Carp interpret this to be a reflection of defensiveness among older
adults towards a situation they cannot change. Moen (1978) makes a similar
observation. She was unsuccessful in obtaining any variation in older
peoples' evaluations of a number of social services. Only after the formal
interview had been terminated, were the older respondents willing to note some

of their dissatisfactions, quasi "off the record." Unfortunately, the data we worked with did not contain any measures that were relevant to the investigations of these and similar hypotheses.

In testing explanations for the age-satisfaction relationship by measures that we had available in a multiple regression framework, we made an assumption that proved tenable in Chapter 5. We assumed that health, income, and education have a similar impact on subjective well-being at different age levels. We found that the impact of these three variables was in fact equal across age levels, thereby justifying the use of these predictors for explanations of age differences in subjective well-being. Parenthetically, it might be noted that marital status may function similarly as these other variables, i.e. act to suppress even higher levels of satisfaction among the aged, since it is a strong predictor of subjective well-being and the proportion of married respondents declines with increasing age. However, we did not investigate this hypothesis in the report.

Predictors of subjective well-being. More generally, our investigations of the effects of commonly used sociodemographic predictors of subjective well-being as well as individual satisfactions with those sociodemographic factors as predictors suggest that predictor patterns do not vary much across age levels. In other words, much of what has been reported in the gerontological literature on subjective well-being--such as the significance of health, marital status and economic satisfaction--applies in fact to the entire age range rather than just to older persons.

Moreover, the two types of predictors--sociodemographic factors and domain satisfactions--do not always show the same patterns. For example, whether a respondent is presently married or not turns out to be one of the most powerful of all the sociodemographic predictors that we have investigated. On the other hand, variations in how satisfied married individuals are with their marriages is somewhat less of a critical predictor specifically among older adults. Similarly, the amount of family income does not show a consistently strong impact on subjective well-being. However, the satisfaction with one's economic situation has a strong impact at all age levels.

It would be very interesting to include satisfactions and roles/resources into the same causal model, conceptualizing satisfactions as mediators of the more objectively measured "availability" of roles and resources. Such models for the specific areas of economic and residential well-being have been proposed by Liang and his colleagues (Liang and Fairchild, 1979; Liang et al., 1980) and Rodgers (forthcoming), respectively. However, while residential and economic lifestyles change but do not vanish entirely when people get older, many of the roles and resources of interest to social gerontologists are lost by many older persons. Typical examples are marriage and work. Thus, in older age the critical question to be examined becomes increasingly "How can alternative sources of subjective well-being be expanded and developed?" rather than "How do quantitative differences in a standard set of sources impact on subjective well-being?"

Alternative sources of subjective well-being for older persons. Throughout this report we have been concerned with identifying alternative sources of satisfaction to which older persons may turn after they have completed major societal duties such as work or raising a family. In fact, older adults mention leisure activities slightly more often as a source of happiness than do younger adults (Chapter 2). And satisfactions with leisure activities and interpersonal relations seem to be slightly more predictive of overall subjective well-being among older than younger adults (Chapter 6). However, these age differences are rather small and therefore they should be interpreted only as suggestive of leisure and interpersonal satisfactions as alternative sources of satisfaction in older age. Moreover, the impact of leisure activities is not replicated when purely quantitative measures of leisure such as participation in or amount of time spent in leisure activities are used (Chapter 7).

Meaning of age differences. It should be noted that any of the age differences in either mean levels or interrelationships that we discovered in our analyses could reflect either a cohort or an aging effect. With cross-sectional data, these two general effects cannot always be differentiated, although the identification of certain patterns or explanations sometimes help to exclude one or the other general effect.

For example, the question of cohort vs. aging needs to be more fully explored with respect to the finding that older respondents tend to display higher levels of subjective well-being. Thus, we need to ask whether this higher satisfaction truly represents a product of aging or whether it represents the effect of particular circumstances faced by this cohort of older people as they were growing up. Following our analyses we have offered a few speculations on this issue in Chapter 4. However, additional measures of potential explanations as well as multiple measures on multiple cohorts would provide valuable additional data to address the question more thoroughly.

Form of age comparisons. Unlike most investigations of age differences which conduct separate analyses for all age levels and then "eyeball" differences, we have made a concerted effort to build into our procedures systematic tests of the significance of age differences. In the analyses of perceived sources of subjective well-being (Chapter 2) and in the analyses of the relationship between satisfactions and age (Chapter 4) such tests consisted of simple chi-square or correlational tests of bivariate relationships. In the age-specific factor analyses of the domain satisfactions (Chapter 3) we used confirmatory factor analysis to test the equality of the factor structures. In the analyses of the impact of sociodemographic (Chapter 5) and satisfaction (Chapter 6) predictors we utilized interaction terms to test the significance of the age differences between regression coefficients. We feel that these analytical procedures have sharpened our ability to assess the level of age differences existing in our findings, and we would like to suggest their adoption by other researchers doing work on certain types of age differences.

Differences between measures. We deferred the decision about whether or not different measures of subjective well-being are equivalent until after the completion of our analyses. After having examined results separately for domain-specific as well as for global measures, and for satisfaction as well as for happiness measures, we offer a few tentative conclusions.

The two global measures of happiness and life satisfaction appear to measure a similar underlying concept. We found that the two measures are highly interrelated and that for the most part they do not yield any consistently different results in the substantive analyses. Moreover, a set of domain specific measures referring to some of the major areas of life predict overall life satisfaction quite well at all age levels. This suggests that where a global measure of life satisfaction is desired, a combination of the domain specific questions could be used as a substitute for single item global measures with a likely increase in reliability due to the higher number of items. Although slight differences in weights of the different components for the different age groups are implied by our analyses in Chapter 6, weights usually do not affect the performance of a combined index enough to justify the increased complexity of their use.

Need for further research. We hope that future research can address some of the issues that our work raised: What are the specific psychological mechanisms that might account for the higher levels of subjective well being among older people? To what degree do cohort differences rather than age differences account for the higher levels of subjective well being among older people? To what degree do resources and roles exert their influence directly on subjective well being and to what extent do they exert it indirectly through satisfaction with roles and resources?

APPENDIX A

MEASURES OF SUBJECTIVE WELL-BEING USED IN THE DIFFERENT STUDIES

Quality of Life Study, 1971

1. Satisfaction from Finances:

    "How much satisfaction do you get from--Your financial situation?"

            7. A very great deal
            6. A great deal
            5. Quite a bit
            4. A fair amount
            3. Some
            2. A little
            1. None

2. Satisfaction with Job:

    (If R is working) "All things considered, how satisfied are you with your <main> job?"

            7. Completely satisfied
            6.
            5.
            4. Neutral
            3.
            2.
            1. Completely dissatisfied

3. Satisfaction with Family Life:

    "All things considered, how satisfied are you with your family life--the time you spend and the things you do with members of your family?"

            (Same response scale as item 2)

4. Satisfaction with Marriage:

    (If R is married) "All things considered, how satisfied are you with your marriage?"

            (Same response scale as item 2)

5. Satisfaction with Spare Time:

    "Overall, how satisfied are you with the ways to spend your spare time?"

            (Same response scale as item 2)

6. Satisfaction with House/Apartment:

    "Considering all the things we have talked about, how satisfied or dissatisfied are you with this (house/apartment)?"

        (Same response scale as item 2)

7. Satisfaction with City/County:

    "I want you to tell me how satisfied you are with (name, city or county) as a place to live in."

        (Same response scale as item 2)

8. Satisfaction with Friendships:

    "All things considered, how satisfied are you with your friendships--with the time you can spend with friends, the things you do together, the number of friends you have, as well as the particular people who are your friends?"

        (Same response scale as item 2)

9. Satisfaction with Standard of Living:

    "The things people have--housing, car, furniture, recreation, and the like--make up their standard of living. Some people are satisfied with their standard of living, others feel it is not as high as they would like. How satisfied are you with your standard of living?"

        (Same response scale as item 2)

10. Satisfaction with Health:

    "Of course most people get sick now and then, but overall, how satisfied are you with your own health?"

        (Same response scale as item 2)

11. Satisfaction with Life as a Whole:

    "We have talked about various parts of your life, now I want to ask you about your life as a whole. How satisfied are you with your life as a whole these days?"

        (Same response scale as item 2)

12. "Taking all things together, how would you say things are these days-- would you say that you're very happy, pretty happy or not too happy these days?"

            5. Very happy
            3. Pretty happy
            1. Not too happy

Quality of Life Study, 1978

The questions on subjective well-being that were used from the 1978
Quality of Life Survey were identical to these in the 1971 Quality of Life
Survey, except that a specific question on satisfaction with income was
available (such question was not included in the 1971 quality of life study).

General Social Surveys, 1972 - 1976

1. Satisfaction with Finances:

    "We are interested in how people are getting along financially these days. So far as you and your family are concerned, would you say that you are pretty well satisfied with your present financial situation, more or less satisfied, or not satisfied at all?"

          3. Pretty well satisfied
          2. More or less satisfied
          1. Not satisfied at all

2. Satisfaction with Work:

    "On the whole, how satisfied are you with the work you do--would you say you are very satisfied, moderately satisfied, a little dissatisfied, or very dissatisfied?"

          4. Very satisfied
          3. Moderately satisfied
          2. A little dissatisfied
          1. Very dissatisfied

3. Satisfaction from Family Life:

    <How much satisfaction from> "your family life"

          7. A very great deal
          6. A great deal
          5. Quite a bit
          4. A fair amount
          3. Some
          2. A little
          1. None

4. Happiness of Marriage:

    (If R is married) "Taking things all together, how would you describe your marriage? Would you say that your marriage is very happy, pretty happy, or not too happy?"

          3. Very happy
          2. Pretty happy
          1. Not too happy

5. Satisfaction from Non-work Activities:

    <How much satisfaction from> "Your non-working activities--hobbies and so on"

          (Same response scale as item 3)

6. Satisfaction from Community:

    <How much satisfaction from> "The city or place you live in"

            (Same response scale as item 3)

7. Satisfaction from Friendships:

    <How much satisfaction from> "Your friendships"

            (Same response scale as item 3)

8. Satisfaction from Health:

    <How much satisfaction from> "Your health and physical condition"

            (Same response scale as item 3)

9. Happiness:

    "Taken all together, how would you say things are these days--would you
say that you are very happy, pretty happy, or not happy?"

            (Same response scale as item 4)

Ommnibus Surveys, 1973 - 1975

1. Satisfaction with Family Income:

    "The income you (and your family) have?"

            7. Delighted
            6. Pleased
            5. Mostly satisfied
            4. Mixed
            3. Mostly dissatisfied
            2. Unhappy
            1. Terrible

2. Satisfaction with Job:

    "With your job?"

            (Same response scale as item 1)

3. Satisfaction with Standard of Living:

    "With your standard of living--the things you have like housing, car
furniture, recreation and the like?"

            (Same response scale as item 1)

4. Happiness of Marriage:

    "Taking everything together, how happy would you say your marriage is?"

            1. Not too happy
            2. Happy
            3. Very happy
            4. Extremely happy

5. Satisfaction with Life as a whole:

    "How do you feel about your life as a whole?"

            (Same response scale as item 1)

Social Indicator Studies, 1972

1. Satisfaction with Family Income:

   "The income you (and your family) have?"

   - 7. Delighted
   - 6. Pleased
   - 5. Mostly satisfied
   - 4. Mixed
   - 3. Mostly dissatisfied
   - 2. Unhappy
   - 1. Terrible

2. Satisfaction with Job:

   "Your job?"

   (Same response scale as item 1)

3. Satisfaction with Things Done with Family:

   "The things you and your family do together?"

   (Same response scale as item 1)

4. Satisfaction with Marriage:

   "Your marriage?"

   (Same response scale as item 1)

5. Satisfaction with Spare Time:

   "The way you spend your spare time, your non-working activities?"

   (Same response scale as item 1)

6. Satisfaction with House/Apartment:

   "How do you feel about your house/apartment?"

   (Same response scale as item 3)

7. Satisfaction with Community:

   "This community as a place to live?"

   (Same response scale as item 1)

8. Satisfaction with Things Done with Friends:

   "The things you do and the times you have with your friends?"

        (Same response scale as item 1)

9. Satisfaction with Standard of Living:

   "Your standard of living--the things you have like housing, car, furniture, recreation, and the like?"

        (Same response scale as item 1)

10. Satisfaction with Health:

    "Your own health and physical condition?"

        (Same response scale as item 1)

11. Satisfaction with Life as a Whole:

    "Now a very general one: How do you feel about your life as a whole?"

        (Same response scale as item 1)

12. Happiness:

    "Taking all things together, how would you say things are these days--would you say you're very happy, pretty happy, or not too happy these days?"

            5. Very happy
            3. Pretty happy
            1. Not too happy

Social Indicator Study in Detroit, 1974

1. Satisfaction with Family Income:

    "How satisfied are you with the income you (and your family) have?"

    7. Completely satisfied
    6.
    5.
    4. Neutral
    3.
    2.
    1. Completely dissatisfied

2. Satisfaction with Job:

    "All things considered, how satisfied are you with your job?"

    (Same response scale as item 1)

3. Satisfaction with Family Life:

    "How satisfied are you with your family life--the time you spend and the things you do with your family?"

    (Same response scale as item 1)

4. Satisfaction with Marriage:

    "How satisfied are you with your marriage?"

    (Same response scale as item 1)

5. Satisfaction with Leisure Time:

    "How satisfied are you with the way you spend your leisure time-- recreation, relaxation, and so on?"

    (Same response scale as item 1)

6. Satisfaction with House/Apartment:

    "Considering all the things we have talked about, how satisfied or dissatisfied are you with this (house/apartment)?"

    (Same response scale as item 1)

9. Satisfaction with Standard of Living:

"How satisfied are you with your standard of living, the things you have like housing, car, furniture, recreation, and the like?"

(Same response scale as item 1)

10. Satisfaction with Health:

"Of course, everyone gets sick now and then, but how satisfied are you with your health?"

(Same response scale as item 1)

11. Satisfaction with Life as a Whole:

"We have talked about various parts of your life, now I want to ask you about your life as a whole. How satisfied are you with your life as a whole these days?"

(Same response scale as item 3)

12. Happiness:

"Taking all things together, how would you say things are these days-- would you say you're very happy, pretty happy, or not too happy these days?"

    3. Very happy
    2. Pretty happy
    1. Not too happy

105

Americans View Their Mental Health Study, 1976

1. Happiness:

"How about the way things are today--what are some of the things you feel pretty happy about these days?"

2. Unhappiness:

"Everyone has things about their life they're not completely happy about. What are some of the things that you're not too happy about these days?"

3. Worries:

"Everybody has some things he worries about more or less. What kinds of things do you worry about most?"

Time Use in Economic and Social Accounts, 1975-1976

Satisfaction with life as a whole:

"How do you feel about your life as a whole?."

7. Delighted
6. Pleased
5. Mostly satisfied
4. Mixed (about equally satisfied and dissatisfied)
3. Mostly dissatisfied
2. Unhappy
1. Terrible

REFERENCES

Adams, D. L. Analysis of a life satisfaction index. Journal of Gerontology, 1969, 24, 470-474.

Adams, D. L. Correlates of satisfaction among the elderly. The Gerontologist, 1971, 11, 64-68.

Alwin, D. F., & Jackson, D. J. Applications of simultaneous factor analysis to issues of factorial invariance. In D.J. Jackson and E.F. Borgatta (Eds.), Factor analysis and measurement in sociological research. Beverely Hills, CA: Sage, 1980.

Andrews, F. M., & Crandall, R. The validity of measures of self-reported well-being. Social Indicators Research, 1976, 3, 1-19.

Andrews, F. M., & Withey, S. B. Social indicators of well-being: Americans' perceptions of life quality. New York: Plenum, 1976.

Andrews, F. M., & Withey, S. B. Development and measurement of social indicators, Spring 1972--Summer 1973 [machine-readable data file]. First ICPSR edition, 1975. Ann Arbor, Mich.: Survey Research Center, Institute for Social Research [producer], 1972-1973. Ann Arbor, Mich.: Inter-University Consortium for Political and Social Research [distributors].

Atchley, R. C. The social forces in later life: An introduction to gerontology. Belmont, CA: Wadsworth, 1972.

Atchley, R. C. The sociology of retirement. New York: John Wiley, 1976.

Balamuth, E. Health interview responses compared with medical records. National Center for Health Statistics, Series 2, No. 7. Washington: U.S. Government Printing Office, 1965.

Baltes, P. B. Longitudinal and cross-sectional sequences in the study of age and generation effects. Human Development, 1968, 11, 145-171.

Baltes, P. B., Reese, H. W., & Nesselroade, J. R. Life-span developmental psychology: Introduction to research methods. Monterey, CA: Brooks/ Cole, 1977.

Bloom, M. Alternatives to morale scales. In C.N. Nydegger (Ed.), Measuring morale: A guide to effective assessment. Special Publication No. 3. Washington: Gerontological Society, 1977.

Botwinick, J. Aging and behavior. New York: Springer, 1973.

Bradburn, N. M., & Caplovitz, D. Reports on happiness: A pilot study of behavior related to mental health. Chicago: Aldine, 1965.

Bradburn, N. The structure of psychological well-being. Chicago: Aldine, 1969.

Bull, C. N., & Aucoin, J. B. Voluntary association participation and life satisfaction: A replication note. Journal of Gerontology, 1975, 30, 73-76.

Campbell, A. The sense of well-being in America. New York: McGraw-Hill, 1980.

Campbell, A., Converse, P. E., & Rodgers, W. L. The quality of American life [machine-readable data file]. First ICSR education, 1975. Ann Arbor, Mich.: Survey Research Center, Institute for Social Research [producer], 1971. Ann Arbor, Mich.: Inter-University Consortium for Political and Socil Research [distributor].

Campbell, A., Converse, P. E., & Rodgers, W. L. The quality of American life: Perceptions, evaluations, and satisfactions. New York: Russell Sage, 1976.

Campbell, A., & Converse, P. The quality of life, 1978 [machine-readable data file]. First ICPSR edition, 1980. Ann Arbor, Mich: Survey Research Center, Institute for Social Research [producer], 1978. Ann Arbor, Mich: Inter-University Consortium for Political and Social Research [distributor].

Carp, F.M. Morale: What questions are we asking of whom? In C.N. Nydegger (Ed.), Measuring morale: A guide to effective assessment. Special Publication No. 3. Washington: Gerontological Society, 1977.

Carp, F.M., & Carp, A. Age, deprivation, and personal competence: Effects on satisfaction. Research on Aging, 1981, 3, 279-298.

Chiriboga, D. A. Life event weighting systems: a comparative analysis. Journal of Psychosomatic Research, 1978, 1, 415-422.

Conner, K. A., Powers, E. A., & Bultena, G. L. Social interaction and life satisfaction: An empirical assessment of late-life patterns. Journal of Gerontology, 1979, 34, 116-121.

Cottrell, F., & Atchley, R. C. Women in retirement: A preliminary report. Oxford, Ohio: Scripps Foundation for Research in Population Problems, 1969. As cited in R.C. Atchley, The sociology of retirement. New York: John Wiley, 1976.

Crowne, D., & Marlowe, D. The approval motive. New York: Wiley, 1964.

Cumming, E., & Henry, W. E. Growing old: The process of disengagement. New York: Basic Books, 1961.

Cunningham, W. R. Principles for identifying structural differences: Some methodological issues related to comparative factor analysis. Journal of Gerontology, 1978, 33, 82-86.

109

Cutler, N. E. Age variations in the dimensionality of life satisfaction. Journal of Gerontology, 1979, 34, 573-578.

Cutler, S. J. Voluntary association participation and life satisfaction: A cautionary research note. Journal of Gerontology, 1973, 28, 96-100.

Davis, J. A., Smith, T. W., & Stephenson, C. B. General Social Surveys, 1972-1978 [machine-readable data file]. First Roper edition, 1978. Chicago: National Opinion Research Center [producer], 1972-1978. Storrs, Conn.: Roper Public Opinion Research Center [distributor].

Dekker, D. J., & Webb, J. T. Relationships of the Social Readjustment Rating Scale to psychiatric patient status, anxiety and social desirability. Journal of Psychosomatic Research, 1974, 18, 125-130.

Deutscher, I. The quality of postparental life: Definitions of the situation. Journal of Marriage and the Family, 1964, 26, 52-59.

Duncan, G. J., & Morgan, J. N. The incidence and some consequences of major life events. In G. J. Duncan and J. N. Morgan (Eds.), Five thousand American families, Vol. VIII. Ann Arbor: Institute for Social Research, 1980.

Edwards, J. N., & Klemmack, D. L. Correlates of life satisfactions: A re-examination. Journal of Gerontology, 1973, 28, 497-502.

Fox, J. H. Effects of retirement and former work life on women's adaptation in old age. Journal of Gerontology, 1977, 32, 196-202.

Friedman, E., & Havighurst, R. J. (Eds.). The meaning of work and retirement. Chicago: University of Chicago Press, 1954.

George, L. K. The impact of personality and social status factors upon levels of activity and psychological well-being. Journal of Gerontology, 1978, 33, 840-847.

George, L. K., & Bearon, L. B. Quality of life in older persons. New York: Human Sciences Press, 1980.

Gergen, K. J., & Back, K. W. Communication in the interview and the disengaged repondent. Public Opinion Quarterly, 1967, 30, 385-398.

Gibson, L., & Klein, S. M. Employee attitudes as a function of age and length of service: A reconceptualization. Academy of Management Journal, 1970, 13, 411-425.

Gilford, R., & Bengston, V. Measuring marital satisfaction in three generations: Positive and negative dimensions. Journal of Marriage and the Family, 1979, 41, 387-398.

Glenn, N. D., Taylor, P. A., & Weaver, C. N. Age and job satisfaction among males and females: A multivariate, multi-survey study. Journal of Applied Psychology, 1977, 62, 189-93.

Gurin, G., Veroff, J., & Feld, S. Americans view their mental health. Ann Arbor, Mich.: University of Michigan Press, 1960.

Goodman, L. A. A general model for the analysis of surveys. The American Journal of Sociology, 1972, 77, 1035-1086.

Gordon, R. A. Issues in multiple regression. The American Journal of Sociology, 1967-68, 73, 592-616.

Hadaway, C. K. Life satisfaction and religion: An analysis. Social Forces, 1978, 57, 636-643.

Harris, L., & Associates. The myth and reality of aging in America. Washington: National Council on the Aging, 1976.

Havighurst, R. J., Neugarten, B. L. & Tobin, S. S. Disengagement and patterns of aging. In B. L. Neugarten (Ed.), Middle age and aging. Chicago: University of Chicago Press, 1968.

Herzberg, F., Mausner, B., Peterson, R. O., & Capwell, D. F. Job attitudes: Review of research and opinion. Pittsburg, PA: Psychological Service of Pittsburg, 1957.

Holmes, T. H., & Rahe, R. H. The Social Readjustment Rating Scale. Journal of Psychosomatic Research, 1967, 11, 213-218.

Hultsch, D. F., & Plemons, J. K. Life events and life-span development. In P. B. Baltes and O. G. Brim (Eds.), Life-Span Development and Behavior, Vol. 2. New York: Academic Press, 1979.

Hunt, J. W., & Saul, P. N. The relationship of age, tenure, and job satisfaction in males and females. Academy of Management Journal, 1975, 18, 690-702.

Jaslow, P. Employment, retirement, and morale among older women. Journal of Gerontology, 1976, 31, 212-218.

Joreskog, K. G., & Sorbom, D. EFAP: Exploratory factor analysis program. A Fortran IV Program. Chicago: National Educational Resources, Inc., Chicago, 1976.

Juster, F. T., Courant, P., Duncan, G. J., Robinson, J. P., & Stafford, F. P. Time use in economic and social accounts [machine-readable data file]. Ann Arbor, Mich: Survey Research Center, Institute for Social Research [producer], 1975.

Kerlinger, F. N., & Pedhazur, E. J. Multiple regression in behavioral research. New York: Holt, Rinehart, and Winston, 1973.

Klein, R. L. Age, sex, and task difficulty as predictors of social conformity. Journal of Gerontology, 1972, 27, 229-236.

Klein, R. L., & Birren, J. E. Age differences in social conformity on a task of auditory signal detection. Proceedings of the 80th Annual Convention,

American Psychological Association, 1972, 661-662.

Kogan, N. Attitudes toward old people in an older sample. Journal of Abnormal and Social Psychology, 1961, 62: 616-622.

Larson, R. Thirty years of research on the subjective well-being of older Americans. Journal of Gerontology, 1978, 33, 109-125.

Lawton, M. P. The dimensions of morale. In D. Kent, R. Kastenbaum, & S. Sherwood (Eds.), Research, planning and action for the elderly. New York: Behavioral Publications, 1972.

Lawton, M. P. The Philadelphia Geriatric Center Morale Scale: A revision. Journal of Gerontology, 1975, 30, 85-89.

Lawton, M. P. Morale: What are we measuring? In C.N. Nydegger (Ed.), Measuring morale: A guide to effective assessment. Special Publication No. 3. Washington: Gerontological Society, 1977.

Liang, J., & Fairchild, T. J. Relative deprivation and perception of financial adequacy among the aged. Journal of Gerontology, 1979, 34, 746-759.

Liang, J., Kahana, E., & Doherty, E. Financial well-being among the aged: A further elaboration. Journal of Gerontology, 1980, 35, 409-420.

Lorimor, R. J., Justic, B., McBee, G. W., & Weinman, M. Weighting events in life-events research. Journal of Health and Social Behavior, 1979, 20, 306-307.

Lowenthal, M. F., & Haven, C. Interaction and adaptation: Intimacy as a critical variable. American Sociological Review, 1968, 33, 20-30.

Lowenthal, M. F., & Robinson, B. Social networks and isolation. In R.H. Binstock and E. Shanas (Eds.), Handbook of aging and the social sciences. New York: Van Nostrand Reinhold, 1976.

Maddox, G. L. Some correlates of differences in self-assessments of health status among the elderly. Journal of Gerontology, 1962, 17, 180-185.

Maddox, G. L. Activity and morale: A longitudinal study of selected elderly subjects. Social Forces, 1963, 42, 195-204.

Maddox, G. L. Fact and artifact: Evidence bearing on disengagement theory from the Duke Geriatrics Project. Human Development, 1965, 8, 117-130.

Maddox, G. L. Themes and issues in sociological theories of human aging. Human Development, 1970, 13, 17-27.

Maddox, G. L., & Douglas, E. B. Self-assessment of health: A longitudinal study of elderly subjects. Journal of Health and Social Behavior, 1973, 14, 87-93.

Maddox, G. L., & Eisdorfer, C. Some correlates of activity and morale among the elderly. Social Forces, 1962, 40, 254-260.

Maddox, G.L., & Wiley, J. Scope, concepts and methods in the study of aging. In R.H. Binstock and E.Shanas (Eds.) Handbook of aging and the social sciences. New York: Van Nostrand Reinhold, 1976.

Miller, S. J. The social dilemma of the aging leisure participant. In A. M. Rose,& W.A. Peterson (Eds.), Older people and their social world. Philadelphia: F.A. Davis, 1965.

Moberg, D. O. Religiosity in old age. Gerontologist, 1965, 5, 78-87.

Moen, E. The reluctance of the elderly to accept help. Social Problems, 1978, 25, 293-303.

Morris, J. N., & Sherwood, S. A retesting and modification of the Philadelphia Geriatric Center Morale Scale. Journal of Gerontology, 1975, 15, 77-84.

Murphy, D., & Foley, J. I'm ok--Maybe. A methodological issue in assessing self-concept. Paper presented at the 32nd Annual Meeting of the Gerontological Society, Washington, 1979.

Myers, J. K., Lindenthal, J. J., Pepper, M. P., & Ostrander, D. R. Life events and mental status: a longitudinal study. Journal of Health and Social Behavior, 1972, 13, 398-406.

Neugarten, B. L. Personality change in late life: A developmental perspective. In C. Eisdorfer and M. P. Lawton (Eds.), The psychology of adult development and aging. Washington: American Psychological Association, 1973.

Neugarten, B. C., Havighurst, R. J., & Tobin, S. S. The measurement of life satisfaction. Journal of Gerontology, 1961, 16, 134-143.

Nydegger, C. N. (Ed.). Measuring morale: A guide to effective assessment. Special Publication No. 3. Washington: Gerontological Society, 1977.

Palmore, E., & Luikart, C. Health and social factors related to life satisfaction. Journal of Health and Social Behavior, 1972, 13, 68-80.

Pierce, R. C., & Clark, M. M. Measurement of morale in the elderly. International Journal of Aging and Human Development, 1973, 4, 83-101.

Pykel, E. S. Life stress and psychiatric disorders: applications of the clinical approach. In B.S. Dohrenwend and B.P. Dohrenwend (Eds.), Stressful life events: their nature and effects. New York: Wiley, 1974.

Quinn, R. P., Staines, G. L., & McCullough, M. R. Job satisfaction: Is there a trend? Manpower Research Monograph No.30. Washington: U.S. Government Printing Office, 1974.

Rabkin, J. G., & Struening, E. L. Life events, stress, and illness. Science, 1976, 194, 1013-1020.

Rodgers, W. L., Density, crowding, and satisfaction with the residential environment. Social Indicators Research, (forthcoming).

Rodgers, W. L., Marans, R. W., Nelson, S. D., Newman, S. J., & Worden, O. The quality of life in the Detroit metropolitan area [machine readable data file]. Ann Arbor, Mich.: Survey Research Center, Institute for Social Research [producer], 1974-1975.

Rollins, B. C., & Cannon, K. Marital satisfaction over the family life cycle: A reevaluation. Journal of Marriage and the Family, 1974, 36, 271-283.

Rollins, B. C., & Feldman, H. Marital satisfaction over the family life cycle. Journal of Marriage and the Family, 1970, 32, 20-28.

Rosenberg, M. The logic of survey analysis. New York: Basic Books, 1968.

Rosow, I. The social context of the aging self. Gerontologist, 1973. 13, 82-87.

Rosow, I. Status and role change through the lifespan. In R.H. Binstock and E. Shanas (Eds.), Handbook of aging and the Social Sciences. New York: Van Nostrand Reinhold, 1976.

Sauer, W. Morale of the urban aged: A regression analysis by race. Journal of Gerontology, 1977, 32, 600-608.

Schram, R. W. Marital satisfaction over the family life cycle: A critique and proposal. Journal of Marriage and the Family, 1979, 41, 7-12.

Schwab, D. P., & Heneman, III, H. G. Age and satisfaction with dimensions of work. Journal of Vocational Behavior, 1977, 10, 212-220.

Shanas, E., & Maddox, G. L. Aging, health, and the organization of health resources. In R.H. Binstock and E. Shanas (Eds.), Handbook of aging and the social sciences. New York: Van Nostrand Reinhold, 1976.

Sherwood,S. The problems and value of morale measurement. In C.N. Nydegger (Ed.), Measuring morale: A guide to effective assessment. Special Publication No. 3. Washington: Gerontological Society, 1977.

Sorbom, D., & Joreskog, K. G. COFAMM: Confirmatory factor analysis with model modification, A Fortran IV program. Chicago: National Educational Resources, 1976.

Spanier, G. B., Lewis, R. A., & Cole, C. L. Marital adjustment over the family life cycle: The issue of curvilinearity. Journal of Marriage and the Family, 1975, 37, 263-275.

Spreitzer, E., & Snyder, E. E. Correlates of life satisfaction among the aged. Journal of Gerontology, 1974, 29, 454-458.

Stone, P. J. The analysis of time-budget data. In A. Szalai (Ed.), The use of time. The Hague, Netherlands: Mouton, 1972.

Streib, G. F., & Schneider, C. J. Retirement in American society. Ithaca,
    New York: Cornell University Press, 1971.

Survey Research Center. Omnibus survey 1973 [machine-readable data file].
    Ann Arbor, Mich.: Survey Research Center, Institute for Social Research
    [producer], 1973.

Survey Research Center. Omnibus survey 1974 [machine-readable data file].
    Ann Arbor, Mich.: Survey Research Center, Institute for Social Research
    [producer], 1974.

Survey Research Center. Omnibus survey 1975 [machine-readable data file].
    Ann Arbor, Mich.: Survey Research Center, Institute for Social Research
    [producer], 1975.

Survey Research Center. Omnibus Survey 1976 [machine-readable data file].
    Ann Arbor, Mich.: Survey Research Center, Institute for Social Research
    [producer], 1976.

Taylor, C. Why measure morale? In C.N. Nydegger (Ed.), Measuring morale: A
    guide to effective assessment. Special Publication No. 3. Washington:
    Gerontological Society, 1977.

Thompson, G. B. Work versus leisure roles: An investigation of morale among
    employed and retired men. Journal of Gerontology, 1973, 28, 339-344.

Tissue, T. Another look at self-rated health. Journal of Gerontology, 1972,
    27, 91-94.

Uhlenhuth, E. M., Lipman, R. S., Balter, M. B., & Stern, M. Symptom intensity
    and life stress in the city. Archives of General Psychiatry, 1974, 31,
    759-764.

Veroff,J., Douvan, E., & Kulka, R.A. Americans view their mental health, 1957
    and 1976 [machine-readable data file]. First ICPSR edition, 1982. Ann
    Arbor, Mich: Survey Research Center, Institute for Social Research
    [producer], 1957, 1976. Ann Arbor Mich: Inter-University Consortium for
    Political and Social Research [distributor].

U.S. Bureau of the Census. Current Population Reports, Series P-60, No. 101.
    Washington: U.S. Government Printing Office, 1976.

U.S. Bureau of the Census. Current Population Reports, Series P-60, No. 119.
    Washington: U.S. Government Printing Office, 1979.

U.S. Department of Health, Education, and Welfare. Vital and Health
    Statistics, Series 10, No. 126. Washington: U.S. Government Printing
    Offices, 1979.

Wilker, L. Towards a convergence in the measurement of psychological well-
    being. Paper presented at the 28th Annual Meeting of the Gerontological
    Society, Louisville, October 1975.

Wilks, S. S. Weighting systems for linear functions of correlated variables

115

when there is no dependent variable. <u>Psychometrica</u>, 1938, <u>3</u>, 23-40.

Wilson, W. Correlates of avowed happiness. <u>Psychological Bulletin</u>, 1967, <u>67</u>, 294-306.

Wright, J. D., & Hamilton, R. F. Work satisfaction and age: Some evidence for the 'job change' hypothesis. <u>Social Forces</u>, 1978, <u>56</u>, 1140-1158.

Zajonc, R. B. The attitudinal effect of mere exposure. <u>Journal of Personality and Social Psychology</u>, Monograph Supplement, 1968, <u>9</u>, 1-27.